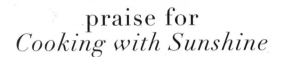

praise for
Cooking with Sunshine

"On this earth the time for solar cookers has (urgently) come.
I have been cooking with the sun for years, and *Cooking with Sunshine*
takes away the mystery and brings the deliciousness and
adventure of solar cooking to the reader."

—MARY FRANK, artist

"A great solar cookbook. *Cooking with Sunshine* captures the fun and convenience
many of us enjoy every sunny season. Where solar cookers can be used year-round
they can save a ton of wood or its equivalent. They could reduce smoke- and water-
borne diseases for 1 billion people on earth, and someday soon they will."

—BEV BLUM, founder of Solar Cookers International
and a solar cook for twenty years

"An excellent book—enjoyable reading, including the excitement
and thrill of actually cooking with the sun—with all the information
plus wonderful recipes. Thank you for publishing this!"

—SHERRY COLE, solar cooking pioneer and cofounder
of the Kerr-Cole Sustainable Living Center

"A complete presentation of simple solar cooking. It covers how, why, and who—
along with a full range of delicious, adaptable recipes. Good work."

—BARBARA PROSSER KERR, initial designer of the simple (cardboard) solar cookers
and cofounder of the Kerr-Cole Sustainable Living Center

LORRAINE ANDERSON AND RICK PALKOVIC

cooking
WITH
sunshine

The Complete
Guide to
SOLAR CUISINE
with 150 Easy
SUN-COOKED
Recipes

MARLOWE & COMPANY · NEW YORK

COOKING WITH SUNSHINE:
The Complete Guide to Solar Cuisine—
with 150 Easy Sun-Cooked Recipes

Published by
Marlowe & Company
An Imprint of Avalon Publishing Group, Incorporated
245 West 17th Street • 11th Floor
New York, NY 10011-5300

AVALON
publishing group incorporated

Originally published in 1994 by Our House Publishing. This is a revised and
expanded edition published by arrangement with the authors.

A portion of the proceeds from the sale of this book is donated to Solar Cookers
International, Sacramento, CA.

Library of Congress Cataloging-in-Publication Data is available.

ISBN-10: 1-56924-300-X
ISBN-13: 978-1-56924-300-8

Designed by Pauline Neuwirth, Neuwirth and Associates, Inc.
Printed in the United States of America

We return thanks to the sun,
that he has looked upon the earth
with a beneficent eye.

—from an Iroquois prayer

contents

preface

HAVE YOU EVER heard the expression "It's hot enough to fry an egg on the sidewalk"? The image isn't especially appetizing, but it does convey an essential truth: we can cook with the energy from the sun. Many of us have been doing it for years by stuffing tea bags into a jar with water and setting it out on the back step to steep in the sun. We just haven't considered extending this method of cooking to other foods.

Until recently, that is. Over the past couple of decades a hard core of solar energy enthusiasts have been experimenting with solar cooker designs and tinkering with recipes. We joined them a few years ago when some solar box cooker plans fell into our hands. We spent a day cutting cardboard, gluing aluminum foil, crumpling newspaper, making a trip downtown to get a pane of glass—and voila! We had our own solar box cooker. We became converts when we experienced how easy, satisfying, delicious, and fun it is to cook with sunshine. Now with this book we're inviting you to join us.

Do you have a few square feet in your backyard, on your balcony, or on a rooftop where you get at least four hours of sunshine a day? If so, you can use a solar cooker. This book tells you how.

Bon appétit!

LORRAINE ANDERSON
Corvallis, Oregon

RICK PALKOVIC
Davis, California

introduction

WHETHER YOU PICKED up this book because you want to save money on your energy bills any way you can, because you want to simplify food preparation or eat healthier, because you're looking for an easier way to cook meals on the river or the trail, or just out of curiosity, your life is about to change for the better. You're about to join a select group of initiates who understand how to harness the most plentiful source of energy on Earth for culinary purposes. You're about to learn to use a proven method of cooking that's good for people and good for the planet.

Cooking with Sunshine is a complete guide to backyard (or front sidewalk, side balcony, rooftop, or trailside) solar cooking. It tells you everything you need to know in order to bake mouthwatering summer meals outdoors without laboring to light charcoal, without worrying about the cancer-causing substances deposited on foods during grilling, and without spending a cent for fuel. In this introduction, you'll learn what a solar cooker is, how it works, and the best reasons for using one. You'll also get the inside scoop on who else is using one, where you can get one, and where the idea of cooking with sunshine came from in the first place. Finally, you'll read about how this book came to be and how it's organized.

▶ WHAT'S A SOLAR COOKER?

A SOLAR COOKER is a device to capture the sun's rays and use the energy to cook food or boil water. Solar cookers come in a variety of designs, from those using expensive parabolic mirrors to those made from recycled materials found around the house. They fall into three broad categories: box cookers, panel cookers, and high-temperature reflector cookers.

A box cooker is a well-insulated box-within-a-box with a glazed top and a hinged lid that reflects the rays of the sun into the box. When the lid is propped open and the box is turned to face the sun, food in dark covered pots in the oven reaches cooking temperatures. Box cookers can be made of metal, wood, plastic, or cardboard. A simple cardboard box cooker can reach temperatures of 200 °F to 300 °F and generally cooks food at around 250 °F. Wood, metal, and plastic cookers typically reach higher temperatures. This is the type of cooker in most widespread use around the world.

A simple solar box cooker

A panel cooker is a reflective panel that directs sunshine onto a dark-colored cooking pot enclosed in a clear insulating shell such as a plastic high-temperature cooking bag or an inverted bowl. The shell lets in sunlight and traps the heat. Food in the dark-colored pot typically cooks at temperatures between 200 °F and 275 °F. The panel can be made of cardboard covered with foil or of some other reflective material, such as metal or the lightweight foam used in auto windshield shades. The first panel cooker was introduced in 1994, and this design has been catching on rapidly. It's lightweight, folds flat for storage, and is the simplest and most economical cooker yet invented.

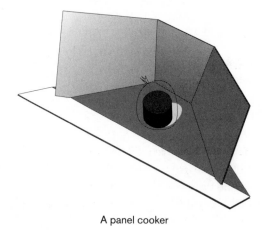

A panel cooker

introduction

High-temperature reflector cookers typically use a parabolic mirror to focus sunlight on a cooking vessel. The focal point of the parabola can become very hot indeed—typically reaching temperatures of 600 ° F and above—in a very short time, making cooking with one of these similar to cooking on a conventional stovetop. Besides a parabola, other mirror geometries can be used to create the focal point: segmented near-parabolas, Fresnel mirrors, and the "three-circle" geometry popular in China. All use the same principle.

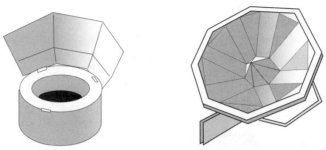

High-temperature reflector cookers

High-temperature reflector cookers are useful for quick heating and sterilization, but they do have their drawbacks: they're expensive, they have to be constantly moved to keep catching the sun, and their high heat can make them dangerous. For one thing, the hot focal point is invisible and can hurt not only the cook but also curious young bystanders; moreover, if not stored properly out of the sunlight, these mirrors can actually start fires.

Inventive solar cooks worldwide have created hybrids of these three types. After you understand the principles of using the heat created by sunlight, you may want to try your own variations. This book focuses on box and panel type cookers because they're comfortably low-tech, easy to make and use, and safe.

▶ HOW DOES SOLAR COOKING WORK?

WE ALL KNOW the wilted feeling we get when we climb into a parked car on a hot day. If the car has been parked in the sun with the windows rolled up, interior temperatures can reach levels that are outright dangerous to living things. Here's what happens: sunlight of relatively short wavelength passes through the windows of the car and is absorbed by the dark interior. The absorbed sunlight turns into heat, which is radiated from the car's interior in the form of infrared energy. But the relatively long wavelength of infrared keeps it from passing back out through the windows, so the interior of the car gets hotter and hotter as long as the sun shines in.

The same thing happens in a solar cooker, with the difference that the heat build-up is encouraged, as in a greenhouse. We position shiny surfaces to reflect as much sunlight as possible onto a dark cooking pot. The pot absorbs the sun's rays and turns them into heat. We insulate the cooking pot in a box, bag, or other shell to prevent convection from carrying away the heat energy.

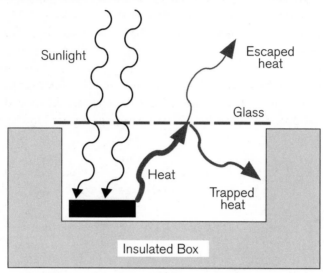

Dark objects in solar cookers turn sunlight into heat.

People are often surprised to learn that most homebuilt solar cookers are made from cardboard. The first question that comes to mind is, Why doesn't the cardboard catch fire? The answer is that the cooker simply doesn't get hot enough. The auto-ignition point of cardboard is well over 400° F, and cardboard is never exposed to such temperatures in a box or panel solar cooker. The highest temperatures occur in the cooking vessel itself; the cardboard is simply there to provide an insulating buffer between the cooking pot and the great outdoors.

▶ WHY COOK WITH SUNSHINE?

IF YOU WERE a woman in the developing world who had to trek three or four hours every day to find firewood for your family and then had to breathe the smoke from a cooking fire in your poorly ventilated hut, you would immediately understand the advantages of cooking with sunshine. If you're a man or woman who lives in an economically and technologically more advantaged area of the world, there are still lots of great reasons to cook with sunshine. Here are a few:

■ **It saves money.** After the initial investment in the cooker, solar cooking is cost-free. There's no need to buy briquettes or kerosene. There are no moving parts that might break and require costly repairs. And because solar cooking is typically done outdoors, it keeps the house cooler and reduces air-conditioning costs. The hot days when solar cooking works best are just those days when you don't want to heat up the house by cooking indoors.

- **It saves time.** Although it takes longer to cook food with sunshine than with conventional methods, you spend less time preparing, tending, and cleaning up. Solar dishes are generally easy to prepare. They go into the cooker early in the day and require little or no tending. At dinner time, when you're tired and the kitchen is too hot to cook in, all you need to do is take a fully cooked meal from the cooker and sit down to eat it. Cleanup is easy because food isn't baked or scorched onto pots and pans.

- **It's healthful and delicious.** Foods cook slowly, evenly, and gently, and remain moist and tender even if left in the cooker after they're fully cooked. The low-heat method doesn't break down vitamins and other nutrients the way high-heat methods do, and solar-cooked foods are free of the mutagens and carcinogens produced by high-heat methods.

- **It's empowering.** Solar cooking gives power back to the people. It's an essential skill for anyone who wants to be less dependent on an increasingly expensive and unstable energy supply, and more self-sufficient in the face of natural disasters and social disruption. It lets you keep cooking in the summertime even in the face of rolling blackouts.

- **It's kind to the environment.** Solar cookers can be made from easily obtained, low-tech materials, and they don't require the use of fossil fuels or electricity. They don't contaminate the air with smoke, volatile lighter fluids, or greenhouse gas the way an outdoor grill does.

- **It's safe.** Most food can't be overcooked. The lower temperatures and lack of flame make solar cooking safe even for children.

- **It's portable.** A lightweight box or panel cooker can go anywhere you go, by car, bus, train, airplane, bicycle, boat, or foot. It can be set up in the park, at the beach, in the campground, or on board the boat.

- **It draws you closer to the rest of the world.** More and more of the world is cooking and pasteurizing water with the sun's energy as firewood supplies are depleted, so learning to cook with sunshine is an excellent way to think globally while acting locally.

- **It draws you closer to nature.** Cooking with sunshine is a practical way to live more in tune with nature's cycles, even if you live in the city.

- **It's fun and satisfying.** What could be more entertaining and magical than putting food into a cardboard box outdoors on a sunny day and taking it out fully cooked a few hours later? Even after years of experience, we find that cooking food with sunshine satisfies something beyond hunger, something in us that likes to be awed and amazed.

▶ WHO USES SOLAR COOKERS?

FROM MANHATTAN TO San Diego, people all over the United States have discovered the joy of solar cooking. The figurative painter and sculptor Mary Frank, a resident of Woodstock, New York, is one of its most enthusiastic proponents. Microbiologist Dr. Robert Metcalf, a tireless crusader on behalf of solar cooking, has eaten solar-cooked meals with his family in Sacramento, California, about two hundred days a year since 1978. A Minnesota woman, Barbara Knudson, uses a solar cooker four or five months of the year and has traveled to developing countries around the world to promote this method of cooking.

As might be expected, solar cooking is best known in the sunny Southwest, where cadres of solar cooks exchange recipes and get together for solar potlucks. (Tucson, for instance, holds a solar potluck at the beginning of May each year.) But newspaper articles have reported successful forays into solar cooking in Minneapolis, Denver, and Boston as well.

We're fortunate to live in a country where solar cooking is more of a lark than a necessity, since cooking fuel is plentiful and relatively inexpensive. This is also the case in other industrialized nations around the world where people use solar cookers, such as Canada, Australia, and some European countries where the climate allows, such as Spain, Italy, Greece, Germany, and Switzerland. But for people in sunny but fuel-scarce regions of the world, solar cooking is a different story—it offers a proven solution to a real and pressing need.

Consequently, the United States and Canada, as well as a few European countries, have been exporters more than users of solar cooking technology thus far. A number of organizations and individuals from these nations have been engaged for a decade or more in demonstrating and teaching solar cooking in regions of the world that are in dire need of alternatives to cooking with wood. Thanks to the efforts of these promoters and of some national governments, programs to encourage solar cooking are in place in perhaps one-third of the countries in the world, according to a survey conducted by Barbara Knudson. One manufacturer of ready-made solar ovens, Sun Ovens International, says that its ovens are being used in 126 countries. Use of solar cookers is particularly widespread in China (which reported one hundred thousand box cookers in use in

1992) and India, where massive government programs have made an attempt to address the problem of burgeoning populations pressing on dwindling wood supplies. There may be more than one million users of solar cookers in these two nations combined.

A U.S. organization called Solar Cookers International has helped to spread solar cooking in the African nations of Kenya, Zimbabwe, and Ethiopia, where more than thirty thousand families have adopted the method. Solar cooking is a real boon to these people, freeing them from the need to cut down trees or go on an arduous daily trek of many miles to find wood. It also offers them a simple way to sterilize contaminated drinking water, thus greatly improving sanitary conditions. And for the women who have started businesses manufacturing solar cookers on a local scale, it's provided an economic boost as well.

Some of the other countries around the world where programs to promote solar cooking exist include Afghanistan, Indonesia, Nepal, Pakistan, Turkey, Sri Lanka, and Vietnam; South Africa, Egypt, Uganda, Madagascar, Nigeria, and Rwanda; the Philippines, Haiti, Costa Rica, El Salvador, Guatemala, Honduras, Mexico, and Nicaragua; and Bolivia, Chile, Ecuador, Paraguay, Argentina, and Peru. A number of international conferences on solar cooking have taken place, including meetings in Costa Rica (1994), India (1997), Italy (1999), and Spain (2006).

▶ WHERE CAN YOU GET A SOLAR COOKER?

YOU CAN BUILD your own solar cooker in an afternoon from cardboard, aluminum foil, newspaper, and glass or plastic—materials you may already have on hand or can easily obtain. In Chapter 6 we explain how. Our solar box cooker cost us about $13 to build in 1991 and it's stood up to almost daily use for nearly fifteen summers. You can also purchase a ready-made solar cooker. In the Resources section we give you information on what's available.

▶ A SHORT HISTORY OF SOLAR COOKING

IT'S FUN TO speculate that solar cooking might have been invented by someone who left a frozen pepperoni pizza on the black dashboard of her car while she ran errands on a hot August day. While this is close to the truth (the Father of Solar Cooking probably got the idea from riding in a hot carriage), the actual history of solar cooking is somewhat more complicated than that. It's an international saga of experimentation by many different people in lots of different places over a number of centuries, punctuated by notable breakthroughs and motivated mainly by costliness or scarcity of cooking fuel. Many solar cooker designs have been tested and abandoned along the way as bulky, heavy, expensive, complicated designs have given way to lighter, simpler, and less costly models.

The phenomenon of sunlight passing through a translucent material to produce heat was probably recognized in ancient times, and the power of sunlight was undoubtedly used by various early peoples. Archimedes, the Greek mathematician and philosopher, invented "burning mirrors" that reportedly set fire to Roman ships during the siege of Syracuse in 212 BC. The Romans in the first century AD were using dark-colored clay vessels to capture and retain thermal energy and were growing vegetables in greenhouses. The Anasazi of the American Southwest (AD 1100–1300) oriented their dwellings toward the sun and must have used the sun's energy to dry grains.

It was the clever Renaissance Europeans who started tinkering in earnest with devices to harness the sun's rays. In 1515, Leonardo da Vinci (who else?) came up with the idea of using a parabolic mirror to concentrate the rays of the sun in order to heat water for dyeing cloth. A French surgeon had a solar still constructed in 1560, and at about the same time a French perfume maker used mirrors to heat water to extract flower essences. A German mathematician with a taste for parabolic curves, Ehrenfried von Tschirnhaus, used a mirror somewhat later to boil water in a clay pot.

But solar cooking couldn't and didn't truly appear until transparent window glass came into common usage. After observing how the sun's rays passing through a carriage window produced heat, the Swiss naturalist Horace de Saussure (aka the Father of Solar Cooking) was inspired to build a small container in which he cooked fruits using only sunshine as fuel. He reported obtaining temperatures of 189.5 °F in a 1767 solar cooking experiment. His experiments paved the way for later investigators.

The English astronomer John Herschel reportedly carried a solar cooker on an expedition to the southern tip of Africa in the 1830s. His oven—constructed of mahogany, painted black, and buried in the sand for insulation—reached temperatures of 240 °F and cooked meat and vegetables. The French mathematician Augustin Mouchot, motivated by concern about his country's dependence on coal, began work on solar energy in 1860, and by 1870 was designing and building solar cookers for French troops in South Africa. His most successful design was a "solar pot" that could bake a pound of bread or two pounds of potatoes in an hour. He exhibited a solar cooker at the Paris Exhibition of 1878. And a solar cooker was patented by a cook for the British Army in India in 1876.

In the United States, the astronomer, physicist, and aeronautics pioneer Samuel Pierpont Langley built a wooden box cooker and used it to cook meals atop 14,494-foot Mount Whitney in 1884. In the early decades of the 1900s, the astrophysicist Dr. Charles Greeley Abbott (who served as secretary of the Smithsonian Institution from 1928–1944) built many different solar cookers, including an indoor cooker heated by oil circulating from an outdoor collector.

In the 1950s, the United Nations took note of the defoliation going on in cultures using brush and wood for cooking fuel, and to address the problem it initiated a study of solar oven designs. During this era scientists and engineers such as Dr. Maria Telkes, eventually director of the Solar Research Laboratory at New York University, designed a variety of metal contraptions for cooking with sunshine. But when UN representatives tried to introduce these cookers into cultures where the need was apparent, they found most people unwilling to adapt. The cookers seemed too complicated to these people, and the parabolic reflectors used in some of these models were outright dangerous. The UN concluded that solar cookers were "a good and useful tool, waiting for a culture willing to learn to use them."

The energy crisis of the 1970s once again spurred interest in solar cooking. Engineers and tinkerers like Beth and Dan Halacy (authors of the first solar cookery book, entitled appropriately enough *The Solar Cookery Book*, published in 1978), Sam Erwin, Bud Clevett, and Ted Owens came up with their own designs. In 1977, Countess Stella Andrassy, a colleague of Dr. Maria Telkes, demonstrated solar cooking as part of the "America's Appetite for Energy" exhibit at the Festival of American Folklife sponsored by the Smithsonian Institution in Washington, DC. (Andrassy later authored *The Solar Cookbook*, published in 1981.)

But the breakthrough solar box cooker that enabled much wider dispersion of the technology—the construction of which is described in this book—was designed in 1976 by Barbara Kerr, a nurse and social worker living in Arizona. Dedicated to the idea of earth-conscious homemaking, Kerr built and tested a number of the solar cookers for which plans were then available but soon ran up against their limitations. They were expensive, tricky to assemble, and small, and they had to be turned often to catch the maximum amount of sun. Kerr decided to make one of her own. "I had a cardboard box and a piece of glass and I put them together and it worked," says Kerr.

Kerr's solar box cooker design can be built with cheap or recycled materials, is large enough to accommodate a number of pots, and because of its broad reflective lid, doesn't have to be refocused during cooking. Kerr patented her design and with her friend and neighbor Sherry Cole established the Kerr-Cole Sustainable Living Center, a research and educational organization that emphasizes solar cookers, solar food dryers, organic gardening, and other technologies that contribute to sustainable living.

In 1987, another landmark was reached when Solar Cookers International (SCI) was founded in California's Central Valley by a group of educators urged on by Beverly Blum, to promote the benefits of solar cooking worldwide. SCI volunteers began tinkering with solar oven designs and in 1994 came up with a design that's even simpler than the box cooker—a panel cooker called the CooKit, made of reflective cardboard. Finally the world had a solar cooker simple and inexpensive enough to appeal to those most in need of it, people living in poverty in degraded natural environments. In 1995, SCI took the CooKit to the Kakuma refugee camp in the Great Rift Valley of Kenya, where residents sometimes had to trade food for firewood, and began its efforts to introduce the technology in Africa.

Solar cooker design will no doubt continue to evolve. A hybrid solar oven with a low-wattage electric backup is now available. A cob solar oven, made mainly of clay and straw, has been built. A solar oven that resembles a cross between a panel cooker and a parabolic cooker and that reaches the temperature of a toaster oven is now on the market. And Barbara Kerr has designed a solar wall oven, a full-sized oven accessed through the kitchen wall so that she doesn't have to go outside to cook with sunshine. Perhaps someday such ovens will be standard equipment in kitchens, at least in the sunnier regions of the world.

► HOW WE DISCOVERED SOLAR COOKING AND WHY WE WROTE THIS BOOK

WE FIRST HEARD about solar cooking sometime after the Arab Oil Embargo of 1973, when energy issues dominated the news. Along with other methods of harnessing solar energy such as photovoltaic converters, passive solar architecture, and solar water heaters, using the sun to cook food sounded like a sensible way to avoid using fossil fuels. But it wasn't until we moved from the Bay Area to California's Central Valley in 1990 that the real potential of solar cooking struck us. We lived in a home in Davis that had been built on principles of passive solar design. Panels on the south-facing roof heated water, and thermal mass in the house helped heat in winter and cool in summer. Our cloudless, six-month summers provided lots of sunshine, and we resolved not to waste it.

When we came across the Solar Cookers International (SCI) booth at the California State Fair, we picked up some plans for building a solar box cooker. We had soon scrounged the materials we needed and fashioned our first cooker from two computer monitor boxes. Though its dimensions weren't ideal, it still worked remarkably well. The minute it was finished, at about 4 p.m. on a summer afternoon, we put a cup of water in a dark pot and placed it in the cooker. In forty-five minutes, the water was just beginning to boil. We were sold! We got the hang of how to cook with the sun by consulting the three self-published solar cookery books in existence at the time, but we soon saw the need for something more comprehensive and up to date. Both of us were writers, and we decided to make it our mission to promote solar cooking to the great American mainstream.

Inspired by the work of solar oven pioneers Barbara Kerr and Sherry Cole, the Sacramento Municipal Utility District (SMUD), and the numerous good folks at SCI, we tried cooking lots of different dishes. Many of the solar cookery recipes we could find conformed to the standard American diet, which is to say that they were heavy on saturated fat and sugar, or else they were vegetarian concoctions that were good for you but nearly unpalatable. We aimed to achieve a cuisine that was simple, healthful, and delicious, and that relied heavily on food fresh from the garden. It took us a couple of years to put it all together and decide to self-publish an earlier edition of this book in 1994, after many of the major publishers had squinted at our book proposal in disbelief.

For the next decade, we peddled the book through the local food coop and through SCI, eventually going back for a second printing. Our personal circumstances changed: we split up our household in 1995 and Lorraine started to cook with a panel cooker that fit her new apartment lifestyle. What didn't change was our dedication to solar cooking and living lightly on the earth. We continued to enjoy the simplicity and ease of cooking with sunshine while watching with dismay as cars and houses got bigger and gobbled more fuel. When the oil price shocks of mid-2005 once again galvanized interest in alternative energy sources, we realized that it was time to do a major revision. Rick went back to tinkering in the workshop, and Lorraine in the kitchen. We added instructions for building a panel cooker and recipes sure to tempt suburbanites away from their backyard barbecues.

Dare we mention our vision? Backyards all over America have solar cookers sitting in sunny corners. The smell of burning charcoal and lighter fluid no longer mars warm summer evenings. Americans enjoy delicious meals that are healthy for them, made from the abundance of their own gardens. They use less air-conditioning because they no longer have to remove cooking heat from their houses in the summer. Fewer mountain streams are dammed, fewer fossil fuel and nuclear power stations are built, because Americans need less electricity to run their stoves and ovens in the summer. A new era dawns with peace, harmony, and abundance for all.

▶ HOW THIS BOOK IS ORGANIZED

THIS INTRODUCTION HAS given you some basic information about the technology of solar cooking. Now you're ready to learn how to cook with sunshine. Here's what you'll find in the chapters to come:

- **Chapter 1** tells you everything you need to know about what you can cook, where and when, how, and in what cookware.
- **Chapter 2** presents an array of simple and fun recipes—from refrigerator cookies to nachos to applesauce to hard-boiled eggs—to try out first thing as a way of convincing yourself that you can, indeed, cook with just the rays of the sun.
- **Chapter 3** contains a full repertoire of recipes for main dishes and accompaniments, emphasizing a healthy diet and including dishes sure to please vegetarians, vegans, and omnivores alike. Each main dish recipe gives suggestions for side dishes to round out the meal.
- **Chapter 4** gives recipes for a range of tasty desserts, including the easiest and most delicious dessert known to humankind, in itself sufficient reason to take up solar cooking. (Check out the Peach Cobbler Cake!)
- **Chapter 5** presents menu ideas for a variety of all-solar and part-solar meals to fit a range of circumstances.
- **Chapter 6** tells you step by step how to build your own solar box or panel cooker using inexpensive materials such as cardboard and foil.
- **Chapter 7** provides answers to commonly asked questions about solar cooking.
- The **Resources** section lists sources of ready-made solar cookers as well as other books on the topic and organizations that promote solar cooking.

Even now, after cooking with sunshine for fifteen years, we're delighted every time we take fragrant, well-cooked meals out of our solar cookers. We envy you your first experience of the wonder and satisfaction of using this simple but powerful method of preparing your food.

1

the abcs of solar cooking

THIS CHAPTER COVERS the nuts and bolts of solar cookery: where and when you can cook with sunshine, what you can cook, what kind of cookware you need, and proven techniques for getting good results. We also reassure you on the topic of food safety, a concern that quickly springs to mind for novice solar cooks.

Before getting on with the details, though, we want to remind you of these immortal words from Ralph Waldo Emerson: "Do not be too timid and squeamish about your actions. All life is an experiment." And so, truly, is all solar cooking. Try anything and everything, and learn from your mistakes. Then share what you've learned with your neighbors. Solar cooking advances by way of such experimentation and sharing.

► WHERE AND WHEN CAN YOU COOK WITH SUNSHINE?

IF YOU LIVE anywhere between the 60th parallels of latitude on Planet Earth and have a few square feet of sunny exposure in your backyard, on your balcony, or on a rooftop, you can probably use a solar cooker. This includes most North Americans, all Central and South Americans, all Africans and Australians, some Europeans, and most Asians.

The closer to the equator you live, the more prime solar cooking days you'll have. On a prime solar cooking day, the sun is high (45 degrees or more above the horizon) for four hours or more. You can probably use your solar cooker for a number of weeks before and after the prime cooking season in your part of the world, but only for easier-to-cook foods.

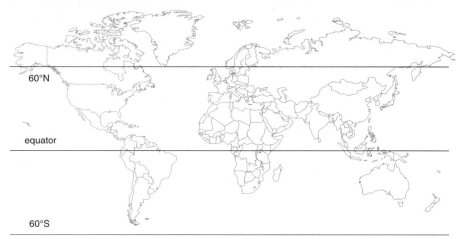

Solar oven territory is the region between the 60th parallels.

The following graph shows the maximum number of prime solar cooking days possible each year over a range of latitudes. For instance, if you live near 40°N latitude—that's the imaginary line roughly connecting Reno, Salt Lake City, Denver, Kansas City, Indianapolis, Columbus, Wheeling, and Philadelphia, as shown on the map on page 3—you have about 150 prime solar cooking days a year, extending from mid-April to mid-September. North of the 40th parallel—in Seattle, Minneapolis, Boston, and New York City, for example—your solar cooking season is shorter but extends throughout the summer months. South of the 35th parallel—in Southern California, Arizona, New Mexico, Texas, and the Deep South—you'll be able to use your solar cooker for half the year or more.

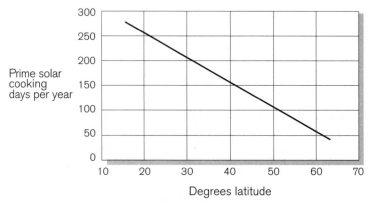

The maximum number of prime solar cooking days per year at various latitudes

Altitude as well as latitude has an effect on how well a solar cooker performs. Higher altitudes typically receive more solar radiation, but the advantage to solar cooking is offset by the longer cooking times required at lower atmospheric pressures.

    cooking with sunshine

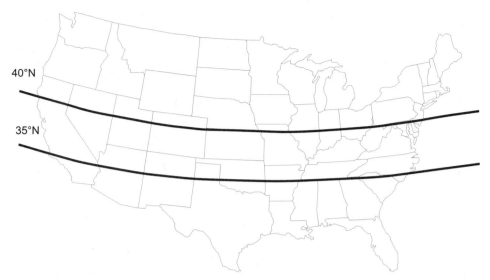

40°N

35°N

The 35th and 40th parallels in the United States. The closer to the equator you are, the more sun you see.

Besides latitude and altitude, there's one more factor that affects how well a solar cooker performs in any particular place—the average amount of solar radiation that actually reaches the surface of the Earth through haze or cloud cover, also known as insolation. When you look at a map of worldwide insolation, you see a few surprises. First, the tropical area near the equator isn't necessarily the best place for solar cooking. The reason is that the tropics experience a fair amount of cloud cover. Similarly, Great Falls, Montana, actually experiences more days of sunshine in an average year than Miami, Florida. Not surprisingly, in the United States the desert West has more

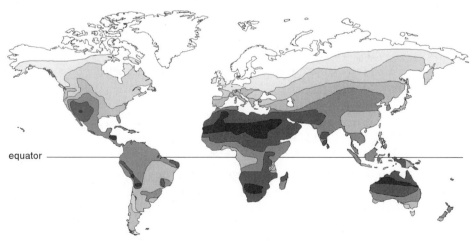

equator

Average solar radiation, or insolation, worldwide (derived from the National Renewable Energy Laboratory, U.S. insolation database)

the abcs of solar cooking

clear summer weather on the average than the Midwest or the East, and thus has the greatest solar cooking potential.

Wherever on Earth you find yourself, your solar cooker should remain unshaded for at least four hours between 9 a.m. and 3 p.m. in order to cook seriously. The hours between 10 a.m. and 3 p.m., when the sun is highest in the sky, are the best ones for baking breads and cakes, and for cooking beans, brown rice, and root vegetables. In mid-summer you'll be able to cook later in the day.

A good rule of thumb is that you can cook with sunshine whenever your shadow is no longer than your height (you and your shadow are the same length when the sun is 45 degrees above the horizon). This rule applies to season as well as time of day.

Another indicator is the UV index, a measure of the amount of ultraviolet light reaching the earth. The local UV index is often available in weather reports, especially in summer. When the UV index is 7 or above—common in summer months—solar cooking is especially effective.

It doesn't have to be hot outside for you to use your solar cooker, but cold temperatures and windy conditions do slow the cooking down. By the same token, cloudiness cuts down on the solar energy available to your cooker and increases cooking time. On hazy or partly cloudy days, you can still use your solar cooker to bake the easy-to-cook foods mentioned in the next section if you have at least twenty minutes of sun per hour. If there's not enough sun to cook your solar meal, you can always take it inside and finish the cooking in your conventional oven.

you can cook with sunshine if . . .

- you live between the 60th parallels of latitude on Planet Earth
- your cooker remains unshaded for at least four hours between 9 a.m. and 4 p.m.
- your shadow is no longer than your height
- your cooker is getting at least twenty minutes of sun per hour on a cloudy day

A word of warning: Don't leave a cardboard solar cooker out on a day when it's likely to rain. Cardboard can't stand up to water. Cover your cooker with a tarp or move it under a shelter.

▶ WHAT CAN YOU COOK?

YOU CAN COOK almost anything in a solar cooker that you can cook with conventional methods. You can't fry or sauté foods in a box or panel cooker, but you can bake cakes and breads, roast a chicken, simmer a stew, or cook foods like rice, beans, pasta, potatoes, and vegetables. The low temperatures are ideal for egg, milk, and cheese dishes; protein isn't destroyed to the extent that it is at higher temperatures. And unlike in a microwave oven, foods do brown in a solar cooker.

After you've tried out the recipes in this book, try adapting your own favorite recipes. Crock-Pot or slow cooker recipes work well. To adapt a conventional recipe to the solar cooker, all you need to adjust is the cooking time and the amount of liquid. Things take roughly twice as long to bake in a solar cooker and use less liquid than in a conventional oven. Most grains, chicken, and fish are easy to cook; root vegetables, brown rice, cakes, and bread take longer; soups and stews, large roasts, and most dried beans take the longest.

If you're adding chopped onions or other hard-to-cook foods to a solar dish, you may want to sauté them on the stove first. We describe this option in the recipes in this book. If you prefer to go all-solar, it helps to mince the onions as fine as possible. You can also bake the onions first in a little oil in a covered dark pan in the solar cooker for an hour or so.

EASY-TO-COOK FOODS (1–2 HOURS):
Fish, chicken, egg-and-cheese dishes, white rice, fruit, aboveground vegetables

MODERATELY HARD-TO-COOK FOODS (3–4 HOURS):
Bread, brown rice, root vegetables, lentils, most meat

HARDEST-TO-COOK FOODS (5–8 HOURS):
Large roasts, soups and stews, most dried beans

▶ WHAT ABOUT FOOD SAFETY?

THE TOPIC OF food safety comes up whenever someone is introduced to solar cooking. The concern is legitimate, but by observing a few commonsense guidelines you can easily avoid problems. We've treated this issue more casually than perhaps we should in our adventures with solar cuisine, but never have we had an incident of food poisoning in more than ten years of solar cooking.

Microbiologists have made a careful study of food safety with regard to solar cooking. They've documented that it's safe to put raw refrigerated or frozen food, even chicken or other meat, in a solar cooker in the morning several hours before the sun begins to cook it. The food remains cold enough to prevent germ growth until the sun starts to heat the cooker. Then the food heats up quickly to the point where harmful food microbes, including bacteria and viruses, are killed—at 160°F, the point where food is pasteurized.

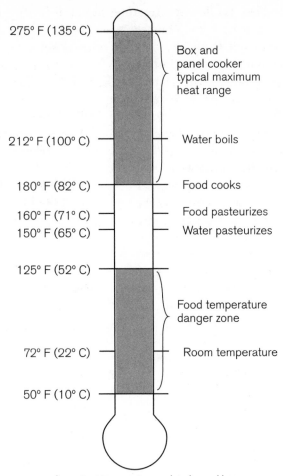

275° F (135° C) — Box and panel cooker typical maximum heat range

212° F (100° C) — Water boils

180° F (82° C) — Food cooks

160° F (71° C) — Food pasteurizes
150° F (65° C) — Water pasteurizes

125° F (52° C) — Food temperature danger zone

72° F (22° C) — Room temperature

50° F (10° C) —

Important temperature points in cooking

Once food is cooked, food safety becomes more of a concern. With solar cooking, as with all methods of cooking, certain bacteria produce heat-resistant spores that can germinate after food has been cooked. Cooked food should be kept above 125°F or below 50°F to keep harmful bacteria from growing. After the sun has left the solar cooker, you shouldn't let cooked food sit in it for more than three or four hours. And you shouldn't leave cooked food in a solar cooker overnight. If food has remained in the danger zone (below 125°F and above 50°F) for less than three hours, reheat it to cooking temperatures with another heat source before serving. If it's been in the danger zone for more than three or four hours, it should be considered spoiled and should be discarded.

Note that bacteria growth is also a danger on a day that starts out sunny and then turns cloudy. Partially cooked food should be cooled to below 50°F or cooked thoroughly indoors.

▶ WHAT KIND OF COOKWARE DO YOU NEED?

THE KEY TO gleaning the maximum heat from the sun is to put your food in thin, dark-colored pots and pans with tight-fitting lids. Black or dark blue enamel-covered kettles and roasting pans are ideal, as is bakeware with a dark nonstick coating. Casserole dishes with a smoky tint also work. Cast iron is acceptable but not ideal, because its large thermal mass means it's slow to heat initially. Cookware that's versatile—that can be heated on the stove when you want to sauté something like onions and then put them into the oven—is a plus. Note that you shouldn't use saucepans with plastic handles in the solar cooker, just as you wouldn't use them in your indoor oven.

Food in many small pots cooks faster than food in one large pot, so pots no bigger than about 2 quarts are best. The most successful solar cooking pots are short and wide because they intercept more sunlight. In addition, short, wide pots will fit into shallow box cookers, which are more efficient than deep ones.

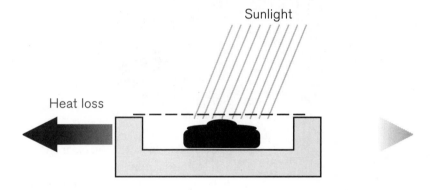

Good — maximum light on pot, minimal heat loss

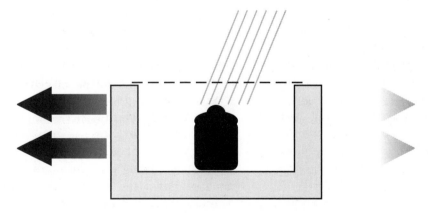

Not so good — less light on pot, more heat loss

Shallow ovens and short, wide pots work better than tall ones.

Don't feel that you need to go out and buy a whole new set of pots and pans, though. You can improvise with just a few pieces. Early on, we baked the majority of our solar meals in a 9-inch-round nonstick cake pan, with an identical pan inverted on top for a cover and clamped to the lower pan with binder clamps. This holds as much as a 1½ quart casserole and has the advantage that we can stack another pot on the flat lid if we want to bake more than one dish at a time in our panel cooker.

Black cake pans make a good solar cooking pot.

Binder clamps, the solar cook's friend

Use the jumbo variety of binder clamps to hold on pot lids, temporarily attach reflector extenders to your cooker (see discussion on page 186), or clamp an oven roasting bag shut around your cooking pot. If nobody's handing you documents with jumbo binder clamps, you should probably count yourself lucky. However, that means you'll need to buy them yourself at an office supply store. Spring clothespins will work in a pinch (ouch!), but the grip of a binder clamp is much more authoritative.

We make do with our clear glass 9-by-13-inch baking pan by placing it on a black non-stick cookie sheet and covering it with waxed paper and then a piece of black cloth. Our clear glass bread pan easily slips inside a brown paper bag for solar oven use. We cook rice and potatoes in a small black enamel kettle we bought at a camping store to use on backpacking trips. We've also been known to bake corn and potatoes by slipping each into an old black sock.

Widemouthed glass canning jars also make good solar cooking vessels. Prime the glass with a paint designed to adhere to glass, and then cover it with a coat of flat black paint. To create a handy viewing strip, put a strip of masking tape down the side of the jar before painting. When you peel it off, you'll have a little window that will let you peek at the food inside. The canning jar is designed to accom-

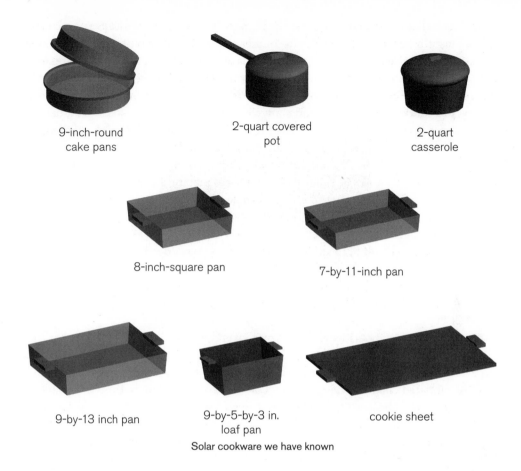

9-inch-round
cake pans

2-quart covered
pot

2-quart
casserole

8-inch-square pan

7-by-11-inch pan

9-by-13 inch pan

9-by-5-by-3 in.
loaf pan

cookie sheet

Solar cookware we have known

modate a certain amount of pressure and release it through the lid if it gets too high. As in a pressure cooker, the higher pressure raises the boiling point of water and reduces cooking time. Avoid jars with standard lids such as mayonnaise or spaghetti sauce jars. Because the lids aren't designed to vent under pressure, these jars can break during cooking.

Tight-fitting lids are a must for cooking all foods except bread, cake, cookies, and pizza, and for roasting nuts and party mix. If you don't cover foods, moisture tends to condense on the inside of the box cooker window or oven bag and cuts down the amount of sunshine reaching the cooking vessel. (You can vent the cooker, something we'll tell you about later, but this cuts down on the efficiency, too.) Exposing foods to direct sunlight during cooking can also degrade essential vitamins. You can improvise lids for odd-sized pans by painting a sheet of foil with a mixture of 3 parts water, 1 part Elmer's glue, and black tempera powder. Or you can use foil or waxed paper draped with a navy blue, brown, or black cloth. You can also put several small uncovered bowls inside a large dark roaster pan with a cover.

One of the ready-made solar cookers available on the market, the SOS Sport (about which you'll find more details in the Resources section), comes with two black enamelware 2-quart pots with lids. These pots are amazingly versatile and may be all the solar cookware you ever need. We've gotten a ton of mileage out of the one pot of this sort that we purchased to use in our panel cooker. You can buy this kind of pot from Solar Cookers International if you can't find it anywhere else; again, see Resources for details.

You may find that it helps to put a wire rack (such as a cake cooling rack) under your pot in either a box or a panel cooker to help insulate it and (in a panel cooker) to allow sunlight to hit the bottom. You can easily make your own wire standoff; see the instructions at the end of Chapter 6. You may also find that placing a black drip pan (a cookie sheet will do just fine) in the bottom of a box cooker helps turn light to heat. We haven't found either to be essential. Some solar cooks advocate putting a dark brick, rock, or tile under the pot in a panel cooker to hold the cooker down in case of wind and, after being preheated in the sun, to apply heat to the bottom of the pot.

▶ HOW MANY DISHES CAN YOU COOK AT ONCE?

YOU CAN PUT as many pots in your solar box cooker as space allows. Just remember that the more pots there are, the more slowly the food cooks. Put harder-to-cook foods and foods in the largest pots toward the back of a box cooker, where the most sun will reach them.

A typical panel cooker is designed to cook one dish at a time but might be able to accommodate two 2-quart casseroles in one oven bag side by side. You can also stack pots vertically in one insulating bag if you have at least one pot with a flat lid. Another way to cook multiple dishes is to have more than one panel cooker available.

▶ USING YOUR SOLAR COOKER

THE GOLDEN RULE of solar cooking is: Put the food in early and don't worry about overcooking. Prepare your solar lunch or dinner when you're making your breakfast. Then put it in the cooker in the morning or early afternoon. Place your solar cooker in a spot that gets at least four hours of sunshine a day. You can place it on a table or platform to make cooking easier on your back, but you don't need to; it works just as well if placed on the ground.

After you put your food in the cooker, aim it so that its reflector directly faces where the sun will be when you want your meal to start cooking. The food will begin to warm before the sun reaches the full-on position and will stay warm after the sun's direct rays leave it, especially in a box cooker. During partly cloudy weather or with lots of food, you may want to move the cooker to follow the sun once or twice during the day if you're around home. If you're baking bread or cake, you'll need the hottest temperatures, so bake between 10 a.m. and 3 p.m. and move the cooker once or twice to follow the sun.

Aim the reflector to face where the sun will be when you want your food to start cooking.

Then forget about your food until you take it out at mealtime. There's no need for you to stir the food while it cooks, although you can take a peek if you're curious. Remember to use pot holders to take the pots from the cooker, because they can get really hot. Putting a brick or two inside a cooker will slow down the cooking initially but hold the heat so that your food stays warm after the sun leaves the cooker.

You'll notice that the cooking times we give in the recipes that follow are quite approximate. This is because many different factors affect cooking times, and you can leave most foods in the oven for as long as you like (although not overnight), until it's convenient for you to take them out. They'll stay warm in their dark pots but won't burn. The best way to get a feel for how long things take to cook in your particular circumstances is to try out a number of different recipes. You'll soon develop a knack for knowing how long something takes to get done.

On a fine summer afternoon, you can put easy-to-cook foods, particularly fish and greens, in to cook as late as 5 p.m. Fish and greens need no more than about an hour of strong sunlight to cook thoroughly, and they shouldn't be left in the cooker much longer than they need to cook. If you're around home, you can put food in the cooker just far enough in advance to cook thoroughly but not sit for much longer than that.

Americans often object that they're too busy to take the time required for solar cooking. We don't know about you, but we hate to have to make dinner when we're tired from a busy day. When you cook with sunshine, you soon get in the habit of preparing dinner early in the day, while you're fresh, and then leaving the rest to the solar cooker. Because solar cookery does require establishing new habits, you might want to start out cooking this way just on the weekends.

One final tip: There's nothing wrong with mixing solar with conventional cooking, as long as both methods are available to you. For instance, you might want to cook brown rice in the solar cooker and forage in the garden for ingredients for a stovetop stir-fry after you come home from work. Or cook potatoes all day in the solar cooker and grill some sausage just before dinner. You can also start solar-cooked foods on the stove, bringing the water for grains to a boil on the stove before putting them in the solar cooker, or sautéing hard-to-cook vegetables like onions and garlic before combining them in a solar-baked casserole.

Regardless of how you eventually adapt solar cooking to your own particular circumstances, we hope that your summertime cooking will be much easier and more fun than before the solar cooker entered your gastronomical life.

2

warm-ups

HERE ARE SOME easy and fun recipes for you to try as you get acquainted with your solar cooker and what it can do. Experiencing success with these recipes will help you get used to the idea that you can, indeed, cook with sunshine.

A number of these recipes call for baking things uncovered on a cookie sheet. As we mentioned in Chapter 1, this is a less efficient way to use your cooker than preparing things in tightly covered pots, because the steam released by foods as they cook can fog up the box cooker window or oven bag. One way to address this problem is to prop the lid of your box cooker open slightly or close your oven bag (if you're using a panel cooker) with a twist tie wrapped around a sewing bobbin or other small object with a hole in it. These measures do cut down on the efficiency of the cooker, but the point is that you can still cook successfully this way.

sun tea

Chances are good you've made sun tea before, without the aid of a solar cooker. Using your solar cooker heats the tea hotter, faster. It may taste better if you drape the jar with a dark cloth to keep the sun from hitting the tea directly.

YIELD: 16 cups

1 gallon water
4 or 5 tea bags of your favorite tea
Several sprigs fresh mint, washed and lightly crushed

▶ Put the water, tea bags, and mint in a gallon jar and cover the jar loosely.
▶ Leave the jar in the solar cooker all day, then cool it overnight outdoors.

frozen dinner

Solar cooking can fit into the busiest lifestyle if you're willing to do a little planning ahead. Pop a frozen dinner into the solar cooker at breakfast and enjoy a hot meal when you come home at lunch, or pop it in at lunchtime and have it for dinner. Or have a child who comes home by 4 p.m. put the dinner in. Absolutely no preparation is required at mealtime. How much simpler can life get?

YIELD: see package

1 frozen dinner of your choice

▶ Take the foil off the top of a frozen dinner and put the container on a dark cookie sheet in the solar cooker. Cover with a second dark cookie sheet.
▶ Bake for 2 hours or so, until heated through.

refrigerator cookies

This is a great way to get kids started with solar cooking, as is the S'Mores recipe. Buy commercial cookie dough from the store, the kind that comes wrapped in plastic like a big sausage. Dark cookies, like spice, chocolate, or chocolate chip, cook fastest. Light ones cook more slowly.

YIELD: see package

1 package store-bought ready-to-cook cookie dough

▶ Slice the dough ¼ inch thick and put the slices on a dark nonstick cookie sheet.
▶ If using a box cooker, put the cookie sheet on top of two bricks, blocks of wood, or overturned loaf pans to bring it up closer to the window to catch the rays, and prop the lid open slightly to let steam escape. If using a panel cooker, put the cookie sheet on a brick or block of wood inside the oven bag and vent the oven bag by closing it with a twist tie wrapped around a sewing bobbin or other small object with a hole in it.
▶ Bake the cookies for 30 minutes or so, until puffed and brown. Watch so they don't scorch (no kidding!).

s'mores

Here's another one that's fun for kids. It always reminds us of summer camp.

YIELD: 4 servings

8 graham crackers
1 cup miniature marshmallows
8 1-ounce milk chocolate squares

▶ Place the graham crackers on a dark cookie sheet in a single layer.
▶ Cover half the crackers with miniature marshmallows and half with chocolate squares.
▶ If using a box cooker, put the cookie sheet on top of two bricks, blocks of wood, or overturned loaf pans to bring it up closer to the window to catch the rays, and prop the lid open slightly to let steam escape. If using a panel cooker, put the cookie sheet on a brick or block of wood inside the oven bag and vent the oven bag by closing it with a twist tie wrapped around a sewing bobbin or other small object with a hole in it.
▶ Bake for about 30 minutes, until the chocolate has melted.
▶ Squish a graham cracker with chocolate and a graham cracker with marshmallow together into a gooshy, yummy, sticky little sandwich.

nuts 'n' bolts

The solar cooker is a great way to roast nuts or party mix.

YIELD: 8 cups

⅓ cup olive oil
2 tablespoons Worcestershire sauce
½ teaspoon seasoned salt
3 cups pretzel sticks
3 cups Cheerios
2 cups salted peanuts

▶ Whisk together the oil, Worcestershire, and salt. Add the pretzels, Cheerios, and peanuts and stir well to coat.
▶ Spread the mixture onto a dark cookie sheet in a single layer.
▶ If using a box cooker, put the cookie sheet on top of two bricks, blocks of wood, or overturned loaf pans to bring it up closer to the window to catch the rays, and prop the lid open slightly to let steam escape. If using a panel cooker, put the cookie sheet on a brick or block of wood inside the oven bag and vent the oven bag by closing it with a twist tie wrapped around a sewing bobbin or other small object with a hole in it.
▶ Bake for about 1 hour, until dry and crispy.

macho nachos

The solar cooker is good at melting cheese.

YIELD: 8 cups

6 cups tortilla chips
1 (14-ounce) can refried beans
1 cup grated cheddar cheese
1 (4-ounce) can sliced olives
½ cup sliced jalapeño peppers
Prepared salsa for garnish
Sour cream for garnish
Prepared guacamole for garnish

▶ Spread tortilla chips on a dark cookie sheet.
▶ Spoon on dollops of refried beans.
▶ Sprinkle with cheese, olives, and peppers.
▶ If using a box cooker, put the cookie sheet on top of two bricks, blocks of wood, or overturned loaf pans to bring it up closer to the window to catch the rays. If using a panel cooker, put the cookie sheet on a brick or block of wood inside the oven bag. No need to vent, because there's not much moisture in this food.
▶ Bake for about 30 minutes, until the cheese melts.
▶ Garnish with salsa, sour cream, and guacamole.

spicy seeds

This is a great snack for hiking expeditions or meandering trips down to the creek in summer.

YIELD: 2 cups

1 cup raw sunflower seeds
1 cup raw pumpkin seeds
¼ cup raw sesame seeds
1 tablespoon soy sauce or tamari
1 tablespoon sesame oil
½ teaspoon celery seed
½ teaspoon cayenne
Three dashes garlic powder

▶ Mix all the ingredients well.
▶ Spread the mixture in a thin layer on a dark cookie sheet.
▶ If using a box cooker, put the cookie sheet on top of two bricks, blocks of wood, or overturned loaf pans to bring it up closer to the window to catch the rays. If using a panel cooker, put the cookie sheet on a brick or block of wood inside the oven bag. No need to vent, because there's not much moisture in this food.
▶ Bake for 1 to 2 hours, until dry.

croutons

Here's a good way to use up stale bread. Keep these on hand to sprinkle on soups or salads.

YIELD: 6 cups

10 slices bread, cubed
¼ cup olive oil
1 teaspoon dried basil
1 teaspoon garlic salt
1 teaspoon nutritional yeast (optional)
Any other favorite herb, to taste

▶ Spread the bread onto a dark cookie sheet and drizzle with the olive oil.
▶ Sprinkle with the basil, garlic salt, optional nutritional yeast, and any other favorite herbs and toss lightly.
▶ If using a box cooker, put the cookie sheet on top of two bricks, blocks of wood, or overturned loaf pans to bring it up closer to the window to catch the rays, and prop the lid open slightly to let steam escape. If using a panel cooker, put the cookie sheet on a brick or block of wood inside the oven bag and vent the oven bag by closing it with a twist tie wrapped around a sewing bobbin or other small object with a hole in it.
▶ Bake for about 1 hour, until crisp.

zweiback

Zweiback, or twice-baked bread, is a very lightweight, crunchy bread that lasts a long time and is ideal as a base for little hors d'oeuvres. Or break it into soups and salads for crunchiness.

YIELD: 10 slices

10 (½-inch) slices whole-grain bread

▶ Place bread slices on a dark cookie sheet in a single layer.
▶ If using a box cooker, put the cookie sheet on top of two bricks, blocks of wood, or overturned loaf pans to bring it up closer to the window to catch the rays, and prop the lid open slightly to let steam escape. If using a panel cooker, put the cookie sheet on a brick or block of wood inside the oven bag and vent the oven bag by closing it with a twist tie wrapped around a sewing bobbin or other small object with a hole in it.
▶ Bake for 3 to 4 hours, until crisp.

bruschetta

Akin to zweiback, bruschetta is traditionally grilled.

YIELD: 10 slices

10 (½-inch) slices sourdough baguette
1 clove garlic, cut in half
¼ cup olive oil
½ cup diced fresh tomatoes
¼ cup thinly sliced fresh basil
1 tablespoon capers (optional)

▶ Place baguette slices on a dark cookie sheet.
▶ If using a box cooker, put the cookie sheet on top of two bricks, blocks of wood, or overturned loaf pans to bring it up closer to the window to catch the rays, and prop the lid open slightly to let steam escape. If using a panel cooker, put the cookie sheet on a brick or block of wood inside the oven bag and vent the oven bag by closing it with a twist tie wrapped around a sewing bobbin or other small object with a hole in it.
▶ Bake for 3 to 4 hours, until crisp.
▶ Rub the bruschetta with garlic, drizzle it with olive oil, and top with tomato, basil, and (optional) capers.

sausages or hot dogs

Take your solar cooker along for a picnic in the park. While you play softball or volleyball or just snooze in the shade of a spreading tree, the solar cooker will be working on your picnic lunch or dinner. It also makes a great conversation piece, guaranteed to draw the interest of passersby.

YIELD: 4 servings

4 smoked turkey sausages, other precooked sausages, or hot dogs
4 hot dog buns

▶ Cut sausages in half lengthwise and spread cut-side down on a dark cookie sheet, along with opened-out buns.
▶ If using a box cooker, put the cookie sheet on top of two bricks, blocks of wood, or overturned loaf pans to bring it up closer to the window to catch the rays, and prop the lid open slightly to let steam escape. If using a panel cooker, put the cookie sheet on a brick or block of wood inside the oven bag and vent the oven bag by closing it with a twist tie wrapped around a sewing bobbin or other small object with a hole in it.
▶ Bake for 35 to 40 minutes, until the sausages and buns are browned.

mini pizzas

Here's a quick lunch that uses up tidbits you may have on hand.

YIELD: 8 mini pizzas

4 bagels or English muffins
8 tablespoons tomato paste
8 tablespoons topping of your choice, such as salami, chopped olives, artichoke hearts,
    diced green peppers, sun-dried tomatoes, avocado, or bacon
8 slices cheese of your choice

▶ Split bagels in half. Place face up on a dark cookie sheet.
▶ Spread each half with tomato paste and sprinkle with the topping of your choice.
▶ Lay a slice of cheese on each half.
▶ If using a box cooker, put the cookie sheet on top of two bricks, blocks of wood, or overturned loaf pans to bring it up closer to the window to catch the rays, and prop the lid open slightly to let steam escape. If using a panel cooker, put the cookie sheet on a brick or block of wood inside the oven bag and vent the oven bag by closing it with a twist tie wrapped around a sewing bobbin or other small object with a hole in it.
▶ Bake for about 30 minutes, until the cheese melts.

hard-boiled eggs

Yes, you can hard-boil eggs in a solar cooker! Eggs are hard-cooked when they spin fast when twirled on a hard surface like your kitchen counter. Until you get a feeling for how long eggs take to hard-boil in your circumstances, it's best to err on the side of leaving them in too long. If you take the eggs out too soon, they'll be soft-boiled instead of hard-boiled. You can always finish them up on the stove by boiling them in water to cover for a few minutes. Eggs can also be cooked in a covered pan without water in your solar cooker. They cook more quickly this way (in an hour or two) but come out discolored and smelling slightly burnt.

YIELD: 4 servings

4 whole, uncooked eggs

▶ Place eggs in a dark pan and cover with water. Cover the pan and bake in the solar cooker for about 4 hours,
▶ Remove and rinse in cold water before peeling.

fresh cream cheese

This cream cheese tastes far superior to the store-bought kind, costs less, and has fewer calories, more protein, and less fat. It's also fun for kids to make. Serve on crackers, English muffins, bagels, or nut breads. Thanks to *Eleanor's Solar Cookbook* for the idea.

YIELD: 1 cup

1 cup buttermilk
1 quart whole milk
¼ teaspoon salt

▶ Mix the buttermilk and whole milk in a dark pot and cover tightly.
▶ Bake in the solar cooker for 2 to 3 hours, until the curds separate from the whey.
▶ Line a colander with several layers of cheesecloth, set it over a pan or bowl, and pour in the milk mixture. Allow the curds to drain for a couple of hours. Discard the whey or save it to use in soups, sauces, bread, or pancakes.
▶ Mix salt into the curds thoroughly with a wooden spoon. Store the cheese covered in the refrigerator.

crunchy nutty granola

After you've made your own granola, you'll have a hard time going back to the taste of store-bought.

YIELD: 10 cups

⅔ cup canola oil or flaxseed oil
⅓ cup honey
½ cup molasses
½ teaspoon vanilla extract
7 cups rolled oats
1 cup raw sunflower seeds
1 cup wheat germ
1 cup raw cashews

▶ Mix the oil, honey, and molasses in a large dark pot and heat in the solar cooker until thin.
▶ Add the vanilla and stir. Then add the oats, sunflower seeds, wheat germ, and cashews and stir well to coat.
▶ Spread the mixture in a dark, shallow, nonstick baking pan in a thin layer.
▶ If using a box cooker, prop the lid open slightly to let steam escape. If using a panel cooker, put the pan on a brick or block of wood inside the oven bag and vent the oven bag by closing it with a twist tie wrapped around a sewing bobbin or other small object with a hole in it.
▶ Bake until dry, about 3 hours, stirring occasionally.

granola bars

Here's something else to pack along on the trail.

YIELD: 16 bars

⅔ cup canola oil or flaxseed oil
⅓ cup honey
½ cup molasses
½ teaspoon vanilla extract
5 cups rolled oats
1 cup raw sunflower seeds
1 cup wheat germ
1 cup raw cashews

▶ Mix the oil, honey, and molasses in a large dark pot and heat in the solar cooker until thin.
▶ Add the vanilla and stir. Then add the oats, sunflower seeds, wheat germ, and cashews and stir well to coat.
▶ Lightly oil two dark 8-inch-square baking pans. Press the mixture into the prepared pans.
▶ Bake uncovered in the solar cooker for 3 to 4 hours, until the bars are the texture you like them (less time for chewy bars, more time for crunchy).
▶ Cut the bars while hot, but cool before removing from the pan.

granola baked apples

Bake these a day ahead for a weekend brunch.

YIELD: 2 servings

2 large apples
4 tablespoons granola
2 teaspoons packed brown sugar
Pinch cinnamon
2 teaspoons butter

▶ Core the apples, being careful not to cut all the way through the bottoms. Place in a dark loaf pan.
▶ Mix granola, brown sugar, and cinnamon. Spoon into the centers of the two apples. Dot apples with butter.
▶ Cover and bake for 2 to 3 hours in the solar cooker, until the apples are tender.

tomato bisque soup

Try your favorite soup and stew recipes in the solar cooker. Soups and stews are marvelous cooked at a low temperature all day long. Firmer vegetables like onions and carrots can be sautéed on the stove until soft before adding.

YIELD: 4 servings

1 (10½-ounce) can cream of celery soup
½ cup evaporated milk or plain creamy soy milk
1 teaspoon butter
1 cube chicken or vegetable bouillon
2 cups chopped fresh tomatoes
Pinch chopped fresh chives
Croutons (page 19)

▶ Stir together the soup, evaporated milk, butter, bouillon, and tomatoes in a large dark pot.
▶ Cover and heat to boiling in the solar cooker, 1 to 2 hours.
▶ Add the fresh chives and stir thoroughly before serving. Garnish with solar-baked croutons.

sun-dried tomatoes

A great way to use that overabundant tomato harvest. Sun-dried tomatoes are delicious sprinkled on Mini Pizzas (page 21), in dishes such as Chicken with Sun-Dried Tomatoes (page 66), in egg salad and tuna salad sandwich spread, in scrambled eggs, and in salads.

YIELD: 2 cups

4 large ripe tomatoes
Olive oil

▶ Slice tomatoes in eighths lengthwise and place in a single layer on a dark nonstick cookie sheet.
▶ If using a box cooker, put the cookie sheet on top of two bricks, blocks of wood, or overturned loaf pans to bring it up closer to the window to catch the rays, and prop the lid open slightly to let steam escape. If using a panel cooker, vent the oven bag by closing it with a twist tie wrapped around a sewing bobbin or other small object with a hole in it.
▶ Bake for 2 to 5 hours, until dried but not crisp—be careful not to burn them!
▶ Put in a jar and cover with olive oil. Store at room temperature.

applesauce

This is the most delicious applesauce we've ever eaten, as well as the easiest to make.

YIELD: 4 cups

6 Golden Delicious apples, peeled, quartered, and cored
Juice of 1 lemon
Dash cinnamon (optional)

▶ Place apples in a dark pot, sprinkle juice over the apples, and cover the pot tightly.
▶ Bake in the solar cooker for 3 to 4 hours, until apples can be easily pierced with a fork.
▶ Mash apples with a hand masher or in a blender at low speed, adding a little cinnamon if you want.

3

what's for dinner?

FOLLOWING ARE RECIPES for fifty main dishes, grouped by principal ingredients, as well as for accompaniments from the grains, beans, veggies, and bread kingdoms. You'll find menu suggestions preceding each main dish recipe. We hope these will give you enough of a feeling for solar cooking that you'll start adapting your own favorite recipes to this style of preparing food.

Keep in mind that the cooking times suggested in these recipes are geared to simple solar cookers that reach temperatures of between 200°F and 275°F. If you're using a cooker that reaches much higher temperatures, adjust the cooking times accordingly. The recipes are also geared to quantities that cook easily in a 2-quart casserole. To double a recipe, cook the food in two different pots rather than in a larger pot, which would slow down cooking times.

Often when a recipe calls for onion or other hard-to-cook veggies, we suggest sautéing or steaming the veggies on the stove to start. This results in a better texture and taste in the finished dish, in our opinion. You can also microwave such veggies to give them a head start.

A word about ingredients: Solar cooking preserves the nutrients in food, so it makes sense to start with the highest quality foods available. Whenever possible, we try to eat what's locally available from organic farmers in season, and in any case we prefer to use organic fruits, vegetables, grains, poultry, meat, and dairy. More and more mainstream grocery stores are carrying organic foods, and with increasing demand are sure to carry more. Organically grown food is good for people and good for the planet, just like solar cooking.

Many people who are health-conscious are concerned about the amount of fat in their diets. We maintain that all of us need some fat in our diets, as long as it's good fat. The recipes here call for healthy fats—olive oil, canola oil, flaxseed oil, and butter. In recipes that call for dairy products, we prefer to use low-fat organic versions. In recipes that call for mayonnaise, we use mayo made with canola oil. And in recipes that call for milk or cream, we use plain creamy soy or almond milk.

VEGETARIAN FARE

A VARIETY OF meatless main dishes can be prepared successfully in the solar cooker, from frittatas and lasagna to stuffed vegetables and vegetable stews. They're quick to put together and easy to bake to perfection. They can be left in the cooker all day without suffering any ill effects.

- Casseroles with eggs and dairy products are especially good candidates for the solar cooker. They cook gently and stay tender. The key is to allow enough time in the cooker for them to set completely—sometimes up to 3 or 4 hours, depending on cooking temperatures.

- Frittatas are easy to bake in the solar cooker. Their cousins the quiches are trickier because bottom crusts tend to get soggy. To adapt a favorite quiche recipe, try substituting a base of bread crumbs for a conventional crust (it'll get chewy like French toast) or try a crustless quiche recipe like the one included here.

- Pizza is a natural for the solar cooker. Try out our Pesto Pizza (page 38) and then be creative with your own sauces and vegetables from the garden or farmers' market.

- Pasta is another story. You can't cook pasta in the solar cooker as you would on the stove, but you *can* use the solar cooker to bake pasta that's covered by some kind of sauce. The key to perfect pasta is to use only the amount of liquid that the pasta can absorb, so that none needs to be drained off. We mix sauce with water to get the right amount. Tossing the uncooked pasta with oil before covering with sauce helps prevent gumminess in the final product. Another technique to try is to heat the pasta mixed with oil in one pan and salted water in another pan for about an hour, then combine the two and cook for another half hour.

- Dishes with tofu and with beans also work well and add variety to the diet, not to mention health benefits.

chiles rellenos casserole

Serve with Spanish Rice (page 85), Refried Beans (page 100), and a salad of shredded green cabbage garnished with dollops of salsa and ranch dressing.

YIELD: 4 servings

2 (7-ounce) cans whole green chiles

1 cup grated Monterey Jack cheese

1 cup grated cheddar cheese

3 eggs, beaten

4 tablespoons unbleached flour

½ cup evaporated milk or plain creamy soy milk

1 (8-ounce) jar salsa

▶ Lightly oil a dark 2-quart casserole.

▶ Open each chile down one side lengthwise and rinse to remove seeds. Lay half of the chiles flat in the prepared casserole. Sprinkle half of the cheese evenly over this layer.

▶ Lay the rest of the chiles over the cheese in a flat layer. Sprinkle on the rest of the cheese.

▶ Beat together the eggs, flour, and milk, and pour over the chile mixture.

▶ Cover and bake for 2 to 3 hours in the solar cooker, until firm.

▶ Uncover and douse with the salsa. Bake another 30 minutes uncovered, until salsa is warm.

grits and chiles casserole

This recipe calls for cooking the grits on the stove before putting the casserole together. You can also place the grits and water in a dark pan, cover, and bake all morning in the solar cooker, then put the casserole together and bake it all afternoon. This dish becomes firmer after being refrigerated overnight, so you may want to make it a day ahead and reheat it in the solar cooker before serving. Serve with Baked Tomatoes (page 123) and a green salad or some steamed green veggies.

YIELD: 4 servings

3 cups water
¾ cup hominy grits
1 teaspoon salt
1 cup sour cream
½ cup grated Monterey Jack cheese
½ cup grated cheddar cheese
1 egg, lightly beaten
1 tablespoon butter
1 (4-ounce) can diced green chiles

▶ Lightly oil a dark 2-quart casserole.
▶ In a medium saucepan, bring the water to a boil on the stove over high heat. Stir in the grits and salt and reduce heat to low. Stir and cook until thickened, about 10 minutes. Remove from the heat.
▶ Stir in the sour cream, Jack cheese, cheddar cheese, egg, butter, and chiles. Pour into the prepared casserole.
▶ Cover and bake for 3 to 4 hours in the solar cooker, until firm.

broccoli breeze casserole

You can start this recipe by steaming the broccoli on the stove, or you can steam it in the solar cooker, but it takes much longer in the cooker (at least 2 hours) and solar cooking robs the broccoli of its bright green color. Accompany with Brown Rice Salad (page 88) and a green salad.

YIELD: 4 servings

2 tablespoons (¼ stick) butter
2 cups chopped broccoli, steamed, or 1 (10-ounce) package frozen chopped broccoli,
    thawed and drained
2 eggs
1 cup sour cream
1 cup small curd cottage cheese
½ cup all-purpose baking mix
1 tomato, thinly sliced
½ cup grated Parmesan cheese

▶ Cut the butter into small pieces and melt in a dark 8-inch-square baking pan in the solar cooker. Coat the sides of the pan well and pour the remaining butter into a mixing bowl.
▶ Place the broccoli in the baking pan in a single layer.
▶ Add the eggs, sour cream, cottage cheese, and baking mix to the bowl with the butter in it and beat for one minute. Pour the mixture over the broccoli.
▶ Arrange the tomato slices on top; sprinkle with the Parmesan cheese.
▶ Cover and bake for 2 to 3 hours in the solar cooker, until firm.

bring-on-the-zucchini casserole

Here's a good one for those times when the garden is overflowing with zucchini. Serve with Tabouli (page 90) and garnish with fresh sliced tomatoes.

YIELD: 4 servings

1 tablespoon olive oil
1 onion, finely chopped
¼ cup chopped red bell pepper
4 cups coarsely chopped zucchini
2 eggs
1 cup mayonnaise
1¼ cup grated Parmesan cheese
Salt
Black pepper

▶ Warm the oil in a large saucepan on the stove over medium heat. Add the onion and bell pepper and sauté until soft. Add the zucchini, cover, and steam until just barely tender, about 5 minutes. Drain.

▶ Lightly oil a dark 2-quart casserole. Combine the eggs, mayonnaise, 1 cup Parmesan cheese, and salt and pepper to taste in a large bowl. Stir in the vegetables and pour into the prepared casserole. Sprinkle the top with remaining Parmesan cheese.

▶ Cover and bake for 3 to 4 hours in the solar cooker, until firm.

artichoke frittata

Serve with Banana Nut Bread (page 129) and a fresh fruit salad.

YIELD: 4 servings

6 eggs

6 saltines

2 (6-ounce) jars marinated artichoke hearts, drained and chopped

2 bunches scallions, chopped

1 clove garlic, pressed or minced

2 tablespoons chopped fresh parsley

2½ cups grated cheddar cheese

¼ teaspoon salt

⅛ teaspoon pepper

Dash hot pepper sauce

Dash Worcestershire sauce

▶ Lightly oil a dark 8-inch-square or 9-inch-round baking pan.

▶ Beat the eggs in a large bowl until frothy. Crumble the saltines into the eggs and beat again.

▶ Add the artichoke hearts to the eggs. Stir in the scallions, garlic, parsley, cheese, salt, pepper, hot pepper sauce, and Worcestershire sauce.

▶ Pour into the prepared baking pan, cover, and bake for 2 to 3 hours in the solar cooker, until firm.

crustless veggie quiche

Steam the veggies ahead of time on the stove, in the microwave, or in the solar cooker. Serve with Tabouli (page 90) and fresh fruit.

YIELD: 4 servings

4 eggs

1 cup sour cream

1 cup small curd cottage cheese

¾ cup grated Parmesan cheese

¼ cup unbleached white flour

1 clove garlic, pressed

1 cup steamed, chopped vegetables, such as broccoli, cauliflower, bell peppers, spinach, or carrots, or a combination of any of these to make 1 cup

¼ cup thinly sliced scallions

2 cups grated cheddar cheese

▶ Lightly oil a dark 8-inch-square or 9-inch-round baking pan.

▶ In a large bowl, beat together the eggs, sour cream, cottage cheese, Parmesan cheese, flour, and garlic. Stir in the veggies, scallions, and cheddar cheese.

▶ Pour the mixture into the prepared baking pan, cover, and bake for 2 hours or so in the solar cooker, until firmly set.

cheese strata dijonnaise

Serve with Southwestern Quinoa Salad (page 93) and fresh fruit.

YIELD: 4 servings

3 tablespoons butter, softened

1 tablespoon Dijon mustard

½ loaf French bread, cut into ¾-inch-thick slices

1½ cups grated cheddar cheese

½ cup grated Parmesan cheese

3 eggs

3 cups milk or plain creamy soy milk

1 teaspoon Worcestershire sauce

¼ teaspoon salt

Dash paprika

▶ Lightly oil a dark 2-quart casserole.

▶ Combine the butter and mustard. Spread one side of each slice of bread with the butter mixture. Cut the bread into ¾-inch dice.

▶ Place one layer of bread in the prepared casserole, sprinkle with the two cheeses, and continue layering until bread and cheese are gone, ending with the cheese.

▶ Beat together the eggs, milk, Worcestershire, salt, and paprika and pour over the bread and cheese.

▶ Cover and bake for 2 to 3 hours in the solar cooker, until firm.

eggplant parmesan

This dish requires a bit of slaving over a hot stove to prepare before it goes into the solar cooker, but don't let that stop you from making it, because the result is truly scrumptious. And when you're baking the solar way, at least you can do the hot stove part in the morning before the summer day has become too hot. Salting the eggplant and allowing it to drain reduces the amount of oil it absorbs in cooking. Accompany with Garlic-Dill Buttermilk Biscuits (page 126) and a spinach salad incorporating fruits such as pears, oranges, tangerines, apples, kiwi, or dried cranberries, and nuts like pecans, walnuts, or pine nuts.

YIELD: 4 servings

2 medium eggplants (1½–2 pounds total)
Salt
2½ cups pasta sauce, prepared or homemade
¼ cup unbleached white flour
½ to ¾ cup olive oil
8 ounces part-skim mozzarella cheese, grated
½ cup grated Parmesan cheese
¼ cup chopped fresh parsley

▶ Slice the unpeeled eggplants into ¼-inch-thick slices. Salt and let drain for 30 minutes, then rinse and pat dry.

▶ Spread ½ cup of the pasta sauce in the bottom of a dark 9-by-13-inch baking pan and place the flour in a pie plate.

▶ Heat ¼ cup of the oil in a large skillet over medium heat on the stove. Dredge the slices of eggplant in the flour and sauté the eggplant slices until golden brown on both sides. Drain on paper towels. Add more oil and sauté another batch, until all are done.

▶ Arrange half the eggplant in the baking pan, covering the bottom completely with a single layer. Spoon on 1 cup of sauce and sprinkle with half of the mozzarella, Parmesan, and parsley. Add another layer with the remainder of the eggplant and top with the remaining sauce, cheeses, and parsley.

▶ Cover and bake for 2 hours or so in the solar cooker, until the cheese has melted and the sauce is bubbly.

▶ Let rest a few minutes before cutting into portions to serve.

pesto pizza

Here's a chance to use some of those sun-dried tomatoes you've prepared in your cooker (see page 25). Serve with a green salad.

YIELD: 4 servings

The pesto:
2 cups fresh basil leaves

½ cup olive oil

2 tablespoons pine nuts

2 cloves garlic, peeled and left whole

½ cup grated Parmesan cheese

The pizza:
1 (16-ounce) pizza shell

1 cup pesto

¼ cup grated Parmesan cheese

4 tablespoons pine nuts

2 cups grated mozzarella cheese

2 tablespoons sun-dried tomato pieces, packed in oil, drained

▶ To make the pesto, put the basil, olive oil, pine nuts, and garlic in a blender and mix at high speed until evenly blended. Pour the mixture into a bowl and stir in the cheese by hand.

▶ To make the pizza, spread the pesto evenly over the pizza shell. Sprinkle the grated Parmesan, pine nuts, and mozzarella evenly over the pizza to about an inch from the edge. Sprinkle sun-dried tomatoes over the pizza.

▶ Place the pizza on a dark pizza pan or cookie sheet and bake uncovered for at least 1 hour in the solar cooker, until the cheese has melted.

stuffed manicotti

Start with uncooked manicotti and thin the sauce with water to provide enough cooking liquid. Serve this dish with a green salad and garlic bread. You can heat the garlic bread on a dark cookie sheet in the solar cooker for an hour or until heated through.

YIELD: 4 servings

1 (15-ounce) container ricotta cheese

1½ cups grated mozzarella cheese

1 egg, beaten

½ teaspoon salt

½ teaspoon chopped fresh oregano or ⅛ teaspoon dried

½ teaspoon chopped fresh basil or ⅛ teaspoon dried

8 manicotti, uncooked

2 cups prepared marinara sauce

½ cup water

► Combine the ricotta cheese, mozzarella, egg, salt, oregano, and basil; mix well. Stuff the manicotti with the mixture.

► Mix the marinara sauce with the water. Cover the bottom of a dark 9-by-13-inch baking pan with 1 cup sauce. Arrange the filled manicotti in the pan in a single layer. Completely cover with the remaining sauce.

► Cover and bake for at least 2 hours in the solar cooker, until the pasta is as tender as you'd like it and the sauce is bubbly.

macaroni and cheese

This dish is especially easy, fun, and amazing for kids to prepare. You can also use this method to cook tortellini, substituting a sauce and toppings of your choice. This is good served with a tuna salad made by tearing a small head of iceberg lettuce into bite-sized pieces, adding a drained and flaked can of albacore tuna, a diced tomato, and a minced dill pickle, and tossing with 1 table-spoon pickle juice and mayonnaise to taste.

YIELD: 4 servings

1¼ cups prepared Alfredo sauce
1¼ cups water
2 cups elbow macaroni, uncooked
1 tablespoon olive oil
1 cup grated cheddar cheese
¼ cup seasoned bread crumbs

▶ Mix the Alfredo sauce thoroughly with the water.
▶ Pour the macaroni into the bottom of a dark 2-quart casserole and toss well with the oil. Pour the watered-down Alfredo sauce over it. Stir to mix.
▶ Cover and bake for at least 3 hours in the solar cooker, until the macaroni is as tender as you'd like it and the sauce is bubbly.
▶ Half an hour before serving, sprinkle the grated cheddar cheese and bread crumbs evenly over the top of the macaroni. Put back in the cooker uncovered until the cheese melts.

veggie lasagna

This takes a little while to assemble, but you do avoid the step of cooking the lasagna noodles beforehand. Serve with a green salad and garlic bread. You can heat the garlic bread on a dark cookie sheet in the solar cooker for an hour, or until heated through.

YIELD: 4 servings

The sauce:
1 (26-ounce) jar prepared marinara sauce
1 (8-ounce) can tomato sauce
½ cup red wine
½ cup water

The filling:
1 (10-ounce) package frozen chopped spinach, thawed and drained, or 1 cup chopped and steamed fresh spinach
1 cup ricotta cheese or small curd cottage cheese
1 cup grated carrot
½ cup grated Parmesan cheese or Romano cheese
2 eggs
½ teaspoon salt
¼ teaspoon black pepper
⅛ teaspoon nutmeg

Everything else:
1 (8-ounce) package lasagna noodles, uncooked
12 ounces part-skim mozzarella cheese, sliced
½ cup grated Parmesan cheese or Romano cheese

▶ To make the sauce, combine the marinara sauce, tomato sauce, wine, and water and mix well.
▶ To make the filling, in another bowl mix well the spinach, ricotta cheese, carrot, Parmesan, eggs, salt, pepper, and nutmeg.
▶ To make the lasagna, in a dark 9-by-13-inch baking pan, layer ingredients in the following order: one-quarter of the sauce, a single layer of the lasagna noodles, half of the mozzarella cheese, one-quarter of the sauce, a layer of the lasagna noodles, all of the spinach filling, one-quarter of the sauce, the rest of the sliced cheese, another layer of the lasagna noodles, the rest of the sauce, and ½ cup Parmesan cheese.
▶ Cover and bake for 2 hours or so in the solar cooker, until the cheese has melted and the sauce is bubbly.

tofu enchiladas

For this easy and hearty dish, you can mince the onion fine instead of sautéing it first. Mincing it makes it bake more quickly. Freezing the tofu first gives it a chewier texture, akin to meat. Serve with sliced avocados and tomatoes.

YIELD: 4 servings

1 onion, finely minced
1 (2¼-ounce) can sliced black olives, drained
1 (4-ounce) can diced green chiles
1 tablespoon minced fresh cilantro
1 teaspoon minced fresh oregano
1 (16-ounce) package firm tofu, frozen, thawed, squeezed, and crumbled
1 (1¼-ounce) package taco seasoning
12 corn tortillas, torn into pieces
1 (15-ounce) can tomato sauce
1½ cups grated cheddar cheese
Sour cream for garnish

▶ In a bowl, mix together the onion, olives, chiles, cilantro, oregano, tofu, and taco seasoning.

▶ Lightly oil a dark 2-quart casserole. Cover the bottom of the prepared casserole with one-third of the tortilla pieces. Pour one-third of the tomato sauce on top. Spread half of the tofu mixture over the sauce. Sprinkle on half of the cheese. Add another layer of tortilla pieces. Pour half of the remaining tomato sauce on top. Spread the rest of the tofu mixture over that and add the rest of the cheese. Cover with the remaining tortilla pieces and the rest of the tomato sauce.

▶ Cover and bake for about 2 hours in the solar cooker, until the cheese has melted and the sauce is bubbly. Garnish with sour cream.

coconut-vegetable fusion

This hearty stew has a Thai flavor to it. The longer you can cook it, the better. Serve with peach or mango chutney, Brown Rice (page 84), and steamed greens.

YIELD: 4 servings

2 carrots, sliced into ½-inch-thick circles

2 red or white potatoes, peeled and cut into ½-inch cubes

1 sweet potato or yam, peeled and cut into ½-inch cubes

1 green bell pepper, seeded and sliced into 1 × ½-inch strips

1 winter squash, peeled and cut into ½-inch cubes (about 1 cup)

4 ounces firm tofu, drained and cut into ½-inch cubes

1 (15-ounce) can coconut milk

¼ cup water

2 tablespoons brown sugar

1 teaspoon green curry paste

3 tablespoons fish sauce or Bragg Liquid Aminos

¼ cup thinly sliced fresh basil

1 stalk lemon grass or ½ teaspoon lemon grass paste

▶ Place the carrots, potatoes, sweet potatoes, bell pepper, and squash in a dark 2-quart casserole.

▶ Whisk together the coconut milk, water, brown sugar, curry paste, and fish sauce. Stir in the basil and lemon grass.

▶ Pour the sauce into the casserole and mix gently.

▶ Cover and bake for at least 4 or 5 hours in the solar cooker, until the vegetables are tender. Gently stir in the tofu cubes and bake another 30 minutes to warm through.

stuffed chard

You could also stuff cabbage, using your own favorite filling. The trick is to blanch the leaves first on the stove to make them tender and easy to work with. Serve with Herbed Carrots (page 113) and sliced fresh tomatoes.

YIELD: 4 servings

2 cups cooked brown rice (see page 84)
¼ cup dried currants
¼ cup pine nuts
¾ cup crumbled feta cheese
8 chard leaves with stems trimmed off
1 (10½-ounce) can cream of celery soup
⅔ cup evaporated milk or plain creamy soy milk

▶ Stir together the rice, currants, pine nuts, and feta cheese.

▶ On the stove, boil a large pot of water and blanch chard leaves until just barely tender, 2 to 5 minutes. Drain and run under cold water.

▶ On a large work surface, place the chard leaves underside up, and distribute the rice mixture evenly among them. Fold in the long edges first and then the short edges, making neat little packets. Place the packets side by side in a dark 9-by-13-inch baking pan.

▶ Whisk the canned soup with the milk until creamy and pour over the chard packets.

▶ Cover and bake for about 1 hour in the solar cooker, until the sauce is bubbly.

ratatouille

Ratatouille tastes best if it's started on the stove and then baked. We vary the ingredients depending on what's on hand from the garden. Salting the eggplant and allowing it to drain reduces the amount of oil it absorbs in cooking. Serve on top of Brown Rice (page 84) and garnish with crumbled feta cheese. Accompany with fresh fruit. Ratatouille tastes even better chilled and served as a cold salad the next day.

YIELD: 4 to 6 servings

1 large eggplant, unpeeled, cut into 1-inch cubes
6 tablespoons olive oil
1 onion, halved and cut into ¼-inch slices
1 clove garlic, minced
1 red bell pepper, cut into 1-inch-long strips
3 medium zucchini, halved lengthwise and cut into 1-inch slices
2 large tomatoes, halved, seeds squeezed out, cut into large chunks
1 tablespoon chopped fresh basil or 1 teaspoon dried
1 teaspoon chopped fresh oregano or ¼ teaspoon dried
1 teaspoon salt
Freshly ground black pepper

▶ Sprinkle the eggplant cubes with salt and let them drain in a colander for 30 minutes.
▶ Warm 1 tablespoon of oil in a large skillet on the stove over medium heat. Sauté the onion and garlic for about 5 minutes. Add the bell pepper and zucchini and sauté until all the vegetables are starting to soften. Pour into a dark 2-quart casserole.
▶ Pat the eggplant dry. Add 4 tablespoons oil to the skillet and sauté the eggplant until it browns and begins to soften. Pour the eggplant into the casserole, along with any oil that remains in the skillet.
▶ Add the tomatoes, basil, oregano, salt, and pepper to the casserole and mix well.
▶ Cover and bake for at least 2 or 3 hours in the solar cooker, until the vegetables are very tender and the flavors have blended. The longer this bakes, the better it tastes.

vegetable tofu pilaf

Here's a very easy one-pot meal for those days when you're short on time. Serve with a fresh fruit salad.

YIELD: 4 servings

¼ cup olive oil

1 large onion, finely chopped

2 cups vegetable broth

1 cup bulgur (cracked wheat)

4 cups coarsely chopped fresh vegetables, such as carrots, zucchini, cabbage, bok choy, asparagus, or sugar snap peas

½ cup sliced almonds or walnut pieces

2 tablespoons lemon juice

2 teaspoons chopped fresh oregano or ½ teaspoon dried

2 teaspoons chopped fresh dill or ½ teaspoon dried

½ teaspoon salt

¼ teaspoon black pepper

8 ounces firm tofu, drained and cut into ½-inch cubes

▶ Warm the oil in a 2-quart saucepan on the stove over medium heat. Add the onion and sauté for about 5 minutes, until golden. Add the broth, raise the heat to high, and bring it to a boil.

▶ Place the bulgur, other vegetables, nuts, lemon juice, oregano, dill, salt, and pepper in a dark 2-quart casserole. Pour the onions and broth over them and mix well.

▶ Cover and bake for at least 2 to 3 hours in the solar cooker, until the vegetables are tender and all the broth has been absorbed. Gently stir in the tofu cubes and bake another 30 minutes to warm through.

SEANFOOD

YOU'VE NEVER TASTED seafood as delicious as solar baked—moist, tender, and flavorful. The key is to guard against overcooking—an hour is enough for many kinds of seafood, so plan to make these dishes when you can be around to check the progress of the cooking. Try different seasoning combinations and fish types besides those suggested here—for example, cod rubbed with fresh garlic, coated with caraway seeds, drizzled with lemon juice, and topped with a dab of butter.

white fish with capers

Serve with Baked Potatoes (page 118) and a salad of lettuce, tomato wedges, crumbled feta cheese, diced cucumber, and pitted kalamata olives.

YIELD: 4 servings

1 tablespoon butter
1 tablespoon canola oil or flaxseed oil
1 teaspoon lemon zest
4 bass, cod, or orange roughie fillets (1½–2 pounds total)
½ cup fine bread crumbs
2 tablespoons capers, drained
Lemon wedges for garnish

▶ Cut the butter into small pieces and melt in a dark baking pan, in the solar cooker or on the stove. Stir in the oil and lemon zest.

▶ Rinse fish and pat dry. Turn the fillets in the butter mixture and then in the bread crumbs to coat completely. Arrange the fillets in a single layer in the pan.

▶ Cover and bake for 1 hour or so in the solar cooker, until the fish flakes easily with a fork. Before serving, sprinkle the capers over the fish and garnish with lemon wedges.

poached salmon with tomato-basil mayonnaise

Serve with Lemon Rice (page 86) and steamed or sautéed chard, spinach, zucchini, or asparagus.

YIELD: 4 servings

The salmon:
4 salmon steaks (1½–2 pounds total)
Seasoned salt

The mayonnaise:
½ cup mayonnaise
1 tablespoon minced fresh basil
1 teaspoon tomato paste
Dash Tabasco
Freshly ground black pepper

▶ Rinse fish and pat dry. Sprinkle with seasoned salt to taste and arrange in a single layer in a dark baking pan.

▶ Cover and bake for 1 hour or so in the solar cooker, until the fish flakes easily with a fork. Check for doneness after the first 30 minutes to make sure you don't overcook. Chill before serving.

▶ To make the mayonnaise, blend mayonnaise, basil, tomato paste, Tabasco, and black pepper with a fork until smooth. Serve a dollop on each salmon steak.

teriyaki salmon

Start this dish the night before, so you can marinate the salmon overnight. Serve on a bed of White Rice (page 84) and spoon the marinade over. Accompany with steamed or sautéed chard, spinach, zucchini, or asparagus.

YIELD: 4 servings

4 salmon fillets (1½–2 pounds total)
¼ cup canola oil or flaxseed oil
2 tablespoons soy sauce or tamari
1 tablespoon honey or brown sugar
1 tablespoon vinegar or lemon juice
½ teaspoon garlic powder
½ teaspoon ground ginger
1 scallion, sliced, white and green parts

▶ Rinse fish and pat dry. Whisk together the oil, soy sauce, honey, vinegar, garlic powder, and ginger and pour into a dark shallow pan just large enough to hold the salmon. Stir in the scallions. Place the fillets in the pan skin side up and marinate in the refrigerator overnight.

▶ Turn the fillets over. Cover and bake for 1 hour or so in the solar cooker, until the fish flakes easily with a fork. Check for doneness after the first 30 minutes to make sure you don't overcook.

cajun catfish

Serve with Rice Pilaf (page 85) and coleslaw.

YIELD: 4 servings

2 tablespoons (¼ stick) butter
4 catfish fillets (1½–2 pounds total)
4 teaspoons Cajun, Creole, or "blackened" seasoning mix

▶ Cut the butter into small pieces and melt in a dark baking pan, in the solar cooker or on the stove.
▶ Rinse fish and pat dry. Dip each fillet into the melted butter and then sprinkle each side with the seasoning mix to taste (up to 1 teaspoon per fillet). Arrange in a single layer in the pan.
▶ Cover and bake for 1 hour or so in the solar cooker, until the fish flakes easily with a fork.

fillet of sole amandine

Because sole is such a delicate fish, cooking it gently with the sun is an especially good way to prepare it. Serve with Lemon Rice (page 86), Carrots Baked with Five Spices (page 114), and a spinach salad with apples, dried cranberries, and pine nuts.

YIELD: 4 servings

3 tablespoons butter
1 tablespoon canola oil or flaxseed oil
4 sole fillets (1½–2 pounds total)
⅓ cup sliced almonds
1 tablespoon lemon juice
2 teaspoons chopped fresh dill or ½ teaspoon dried
Lemon wedges for garnish

▶ Cut 1 tablespoon of the butter into small pieces and melt in a dark baking pan, in the solar cooker or on the stove. Stir in the oil.

▶ Rinse the fish and pat dry. Turn the fillets in the butter mixture and arrange in a single layer in the pan.

▶ Cover and bake for 1 hour or so in the solar cooker, until the fish flakes easily with a fork. Check for doneness after the first 30 minutes to make sure you don't overcook.

▶ Cut up 2 tablespoons of butter in a small dark baking pan; mix in the almonds, lemon juice, and dill, and place in the solar cooker to melt and warm through.

▶ Before serving, sprinkle the almond mixture over the fish. Garnish with lemon wedges.

shrimp with prosciutto and basil

Here's an elegant meal that takes a little more preparation time. Serve on a bed of Couscous Salad (page 89) and accompany with sliced garden tomatoes.

YIELD: 4 servings

½ cup dry white wine
¼ cup balsamic vinegar
2 tablespoons olive oil
2 cloves garlic, pressed
10 thin slices prosciutto
20 basil leaves, rinsed and drained
20 large shrimp, uncooked, shelled, and deveined

▶ In a dark baking pan, mix the wine, vinegar, oil, and garlic.
▶ Cut the prosciutto slices in half lengthwise. Lay one basil leaf against a shrimp; roll the meat around the shrimp and basil. Place in the marinade. Repeat to wrap all the shrimp.
▶ Cover and bake for 1 hour or so in the solar cooker, until the shrimp turn pink.

scallops with mushrooms and shallots

This dish is on the rich side, for a special occasion. Serve with Confetti Rice (page 87) and Sesame Spinach (page 120) or with a salad of spinach, orange slices, and kiwi fruit slices.

YIELD: 4 servings

20 large sea scallops
6 tablespoons (¾ stick) butter
8 ounces white button mushrooms, sliced
4 small shallots, minced
½ cup dry white wine
1 tablespoon white wine vinegar
1 tablespoon water
2 tablespoons lemon juice
1 teaspoon soy sauce or tamari
Pinch curry powder

▶ Place the scallops in a single layer in a dark baking pan. Cover and bake for 1 hour or so in the solar cooker, until opaque and white.

▶ Meanwhile, heat 2 tablespoons butter in a medium skillet over medium heat on the stove and sauté the mushrooms until tender.

▶ In another small skillet on the stove, combine the shallots, wine, vinegar, and water. Bring to a boil over high heat and cook until almost all the liquid has evaporated, about 2 minutes. Reduce heat to low and add 4 tablespoons butter, stirring while it melts. Add lemon juice, soy sauce, and curry powder.

▶ Spoon half of the sauce onto plates, place five scallops on each plate, distribute the mushrooms over the scallops, and spoon on the rest of the sauce.

crustless crab quiche

This recipe is adapted from one concocted by the Whispering Pines Bed and Breakfast in Atwood Lake, Ohio. Serve with a green salad and sliced fresh tomatoes.

YIELD: 4 servings

4 eggs
1 cup sour cream
1 cup small curd cottage cheese
¾ cup grated Parmesan cheese
¼ cup unbleached white flour
Pinch of nutmeg
¾ cup shredded crab meat
¼ cup thinly sliced scallions
2 cups grated Monterey Jack cheese

▶ Lightly oil an 8-inch-square or 9-inch-round baking pan.
▶ In a large bowl, beat together the eggs, sour cream, cottage cheese, Parmesan cheese, flour, and nutmeg. Stir in the crab, scallions, and Jack cheese. Pour the mixture into the prepared pan.
▶ Cover and bake for 2 hours or so in the solar cooker, until firmly set.

POULTRY

POULTRY BAKED IN the solar cooker, just like fish, comes out moist, tender, and flavorful. There's no better or easier method for cooking chicken or turkey that will later be used in a salad or in a casserole that calls for precooked poultry. In these cases, you can cook the chicken or turkey either the day before or the morning before you plan to use it. Try this method with any of your favorite recipes that use precooked poultry:

▶ Rinse boned and skinned chicken or turkey breasts or thighs under cold running water, pat dry with a paper towel, and place in a dark pan. Cover and bake for 1 to 2 hours in the solar cooker, until no longer pink. Remove, cool, and shred. Refrigerate until used.

Recipes that call for chicken to bake in some kind of sauce or marinade are also great candidates for the solar cooker. Solar-baked chicken releases lots of juices, so you need to allow for this in your recipes. If you want any sauce you cover the chicken with to remain thick, it's a good idea to bake the chicken for an hour and then drain off the juices (reserving for recipes that call for chicken broth) before adding the sauce. That's what we recommend in our recipes.

You can also try your favorite chicken stew recipes in the solar cooker, because they're sure to work well. Again, cut down on the liquid slightly to allow for the juices released by the chicken.

chicken salad véronique

Serve on a bed of iceberg lettuce and garnish with sliced tomatoes fresh from the garden. Accompany with Zucchini Nut Bread (page 128).

YIELD: 4 servings

½ cup plain yogurt
½ cup mayonnaise
2 teaspoons chopped fresh thyme or ½ teaspoon dried
¼ teaspoon salt
3 cups cooked and shredded chicken (see page 56)
1 cup green seedless grapes, halved
½ cup sliced almonds

▶ Whisk the yogurt, mayonnaise, thyme, and salt together in a small bowl. Pour over the shredded chicken in a larger bowl.
▶ Add the grapes and almonds and toss well.

bulgur chicken salad

Serve on a bed of romaine lettuce. Can be served chilled but tastes best if served immediately at room temperature. Accompany with sliced tomatoes and a green salad.

YIELD: 4 servings

2½ cups cooked bulgur (see page 89)
2 cups cooked and shredded chicken (see page 56)
4 scallions, thinly sliced
½ cup chopped fresh parsley
⅓ cup pine nuts
¼ cup dried currants
½ teaspoon lemon zest
½ teaspoon paprika
½ teaspoon ground cumin
½ teaspoon ground coriander
½ teaspoon salt
2 tablespoons lemon juice
⅓ cup olive oil

▶ In a large bowl, toss together the bulgur, chicken, scallions, parsley, pine nuts, and currants.

▶ In a smaller bowl, whisk together the lemon zest, paprika, cumin, coriander, salt, lemon juice, and olive oil. Pour over the salad and stir thoroughly.

curry chicken salad

Serve on a bed of iceberg lettuce and garnish with sliced tomatoes fresh from the garden. Accompany with Apricot Nut Bread (page 130).

YIELD: 4 servings

2 cups cooked and shredded chicken (see page 56)
1 (8-ounce) can sliced water chestnuts, drained
½ cup golden raisins
1½ cups chow mein noodles
2 scallions, thinly sliced
1 tablespoon curry powder
½ cup plain yogurt
½ cup mayonnaise

▶ Place the chicken in a large bowl. Add the water chestnuts, raisins, noodles, and scallions.

▶ Whisk the curry powder, yogurt, and mayonnaise together in a small bowl. Pour over the salad and toss well.

chinese chicken salad

Accompany with Banana Nut Bread (page 129).

YIELD: 4 servings

2 cups cooked and shredded chicken (see page 56)
1 medium head napa (Chinese) cabbage, shredded
1 package ramen noodles, broken into small chunks
½ cup slivered almonds
1 tablespoon sesame seed
6 scallions, thinly sliced
½ cup rice vinegar or cider vinegar
½ cup canola oil or flaxseed oil
¼ cup firmly packed brown sugar
1 tablespoon soy sauce
½ teaspoon black pepper
½ teaspoon sesame oil

▶ Place the chicken and cabbage in a large bowl. Add the ramen noodles, almonds, sesame seeds, and scallions.
▶ In a small bowl, stir together the vinegar, oil, brown sugar, soy sauce, pepper, and sesame oil. Pour over the salad and toss to coat.

chicken divan

Steam the broccoli beforehand, on the stove, in the microwave, or in the solar cooker. Serve over White Rice (page 84) and accompany with Baked Tomatoes (page 123) and a fruit salad.

YIELD: 4 servings

1 (10½-ounce) can cream of chicken soup
1 tablespoon lemon juice
½ cup mayonnaise
¼ teaspoon curry powder
3 cups cooked and shredded chicken (see page 56)
½ bunch broccoli, chopped and steamed
¼ cup grated cheddar cheese
Seasoned bread crumbs or croutons (page 19)

▶ Combine soup, lemon juice, mayonnaise, and curry powder in a blender and blend until smooth.
▶ Lightly oil a dark 2-quart casserole. Layer half the broccoli, half the chicken, and half the sauce, and repeat. Sprinkle cheese and bread crumbs on top.
▶ Cover and bake for 1 to 2 hours in the solar cooker, until the cheese has melted and the sauce is bubbly.

chilaquiles

Chilaquiles is traditionally made to use up stale tortillas, but fresh ones will do! Serve with Spanish Rice (page 85), Refried Beans (page 100), and a salad of shredded green cabbage garnished with dollops of salsa and ranch dressing.

YIELD: 4 servings

1 clove garlic, minced or pressed

1 small onion, finely minced

1 (14-ounce) can diced tomatoes, or 2–3 fresh tomatoes, diced

1 (7-ounce) can diced green chiles

1 teaspoon dried oregano

½ teaspoon ground cumin

¼ teaspoon chili powder

¼ teaspoon salt

2 cups cooked and shredded chicken (see page 56)

6 cups tortilla chips, or stale corn tortillas cut to chip size

1½ cups grated Monterey Jack cheese

½ cup grated Parmesan cheese

½ cup sour cream or plain yogurt

1 tablespoon unbleached white flour

Chopped fresh cilantro for garnish

▶ Mix together the garlic, onion, tomatoes, chiles, oregano, cumin, chili powder, and salt.

▶ Lightly oil a dark 2-quart casserole. Place the shredded chicken and half the chips in the bottom of the prepared casserole. Top with half the chili mix, half the Jack cheese, and half the Parmesan.

▶ Mix the sour cream or yogurt with the flour. Spread over the bottom layer, then add the remaining chips, chili mix, and cheese.

▶ Cover and bake for 1 to 2 hours in the solar cooker, until the cheese has melted. Garnish with fresh cilantro.

chicken yogurt enchilada casserole

Garnish with sliced avocado and serve with Spanish Rice (page 85), Refried Beans (page 100), and a green salad.

YIELD: 4 servings

2 tablespoons (¼ stick) butter
¼ cup unbleached white flour
1½ cups chicken broth
½ cup plain yogurt
1 (7-ounce) can diced green chiles
8 (6-inch) corn tortillas, cut into 1-inch strips
3 cups cooked and shredded chicken (see page 56)
1 (4-ounce) can sliced olives
1½ cups grated Monterey Jack cheese
2 scallions, thinly sliced
Sliced avocado for garnish

▶ To make the sauce, melt the butter in a 2-quart saucepan on the stove over medium heat. Add the flour and stir until bubbly. Whisk in the broth, raise the heat to high, and stir until boiling. Remove from heat and stir in the yogurt and chiles.

▶ Cover the bottom of a dark 9-by-13-inch baking pan with one-third of the sauce. Scatter half of the tortilla strips over the sauce, then cover evenly with the shredded chicken, the olives, most of the cheese, and another one-third of the sauce. Top with the remaining tortilla strips, sauce, and cheese.

▶ Cover and bake for 1 to 2 hours in the solar cooker, until the cheese has melted. Sprinkle with scallions before serving.

chicken mole tostadas

These tostadas are a meal in themselves. You can also use the chicken mole to make enchiladas—stuff it into corn tortillas, cover with enchilada sauce and cheese, and bake in the solar cooker until the cheese melts. Or serve it over Basic Polenta (page 96) cooled and cut into squares, with a green salad on the side.

YIELD: 4 servings

1 tablespoon chili powder
1 teaspoon ground cumin
½ teaspoon ground cinnamon
2 tablespoons olive oil
1 (14-ounce) can stewed tomatoes, with juice
½ ounce unsweetened chocolate
3 cups cooked and shredded chicken (see page 56)
1 (14-ounce) can refried beans
4 corn tortillas
2 cups shredded lettuce
1 cup shredded cheddar cheese
Cilantro sprigs for garnish
Sour cream for garnish
Sliced avocados for garnish

▶ In a dark 2-quart casserole, mix the chili powder, cumin, cinnamon, oil, tomatoes, and chocolate. Add the shredded chicken and mix well.
▶ Cover and bake for at least 1 hour in the solar cooker, until the chocolate melts. Stir well.
▶ Spread the tortillas with refried beans and top with lettuce, mole mixture, and grated cheese.
▶ Garnish with cilantro, sour cream, and sliced avocados.

margarita chicken

Garnish with cilantro and lime wedges and serve with Black Beans (page 99) and sliced avocado.

YIELD: 4 servings

2 tablespoons canola oil or flaxseed oil

2 tablespoons lime juice

1 teaspoon honey

4 boneless and skinless chicken breast halves (1½ to 2 pounds total)

½ cup finely crushed tortilla chips

1 (14½ ounce) can Mexican-style stewed tomatoes

2 tablespoons chopped cilantro

⅓ cup grated Monterey Jack cheese

Cilantro sprigs for garnish

Lime wedges for garnish

► Mix the oil, lime juice, and honey in a dark pan. Roll the chicken breasts in the mixture and then in the tortilla chips to coat. Arrange in a single layer in the pan.

► Cover and bake for about 2 hours in the solar cooker, until the chicken is no longer pink.

► Drain the tomatoes and puree them with 2 tablespoons cilantro.

► Top the chicken with the tomato puree and the grated Jack cheese. Put it back in the cooker until the cheese melts.

► Garnish with cilantro sprigs and lime wedges.

chicken with sun-dried tomatoes

Here's a chance to use some of those sun-dried tomatoes you've prepared in your solar cooker (see page 25). Serve this dish on a bed of Bulgur (page 89) and accompany with steamed spinach or chard.

YIELD: 4 servings

4 boneless and skinless chicken breast halves (1½ to 2 pounds total)
2 cloves garlic, pressed
1 large shallot, sliced
1 teaspoon olive oil
¼ cup dry white wine
1 cup heavy cream or plain creamy soy milk
1 teaspoon capers, drained
½ teaspoon minced fresh basil or marjoram
¼ cup sun-dried tomatoes in oil, drained and chopped

▶ Rinse the chicken breasts under cold running water, pat dry with a paper towel, and place in a dark 2-quart casserole. Cover and bake for an hour in the solar cooker.

▶ Meanwhile, warm the oil in a medium saucepan on the stove over medium heat. Add the garlic and shallots and sauté until soft. Add the wine and cook until it bubbles. Then add the cream, capers, basil, and sun-dried tomatoes, and stir thoroughly.

▶ Bring the chicken breasts inside and drain off the liquid. Pour the cream sauce over the chicken breasts.

▶ Cover and bake for another hour in the solar cooker, until the sauce is bubbly.

solarcue chicken

Try this recipe for your next backyard barbecue or picnic in the park. While you play softball or volleyball or just snooze in the shade of a spreading tree, the solar cooker can be working on your lunch or dinner. Serve with Corn on the Cob (page 114) and Aunt Helen's Potato Salad (page 120), along with a green salad.

YIELD: 4 servings

1½ to 2 pounds boneless and skinless chicken breasts or thighs
2 tablespoons molasses
2 tablespoons prepared mustard
2 tablespoons apple cider vinegar or white vinegar
2 tablespoons ketchup

▶ Rinse the chicken under cold running water, pat dry with a paper towel, and place in a dark 2-quart casserole. Cover and bake for an hour in the solar cooker. Bring inside and drain off the liquid.
▶ In a bowl, mix the molasses, mustard, vinegar, and ketchup, and pour over the chicken. Turn to coat.
▶ Cover and bake for another hour in the solar cooker, until the dish is steaming hot.

chicken breast roll-ups

This elegant dish requires a little more preparation, so you might want to save it for the week-end. Garnish with chives and serve with Rosemary Rice (page 86), Baked Acorn Squash (page 121), and a green salad.

YIELD: 4 servings

4 boneless and skinless chicken breast halves (1½ to 2 pounds total)
8 slices prosciutto or deli ham
8 slices Jarlsberg or Swiss cheese or 4 tablespoons herbed soft cheese
2 tablespoons chopped fresh chives, plus more for garnish
Black pepper
¼ cup Dijon mustard
1 tablespoon dry white wine
1 cup heavy cream or plain creamy soy milk
Salt

▶ Rinse the chicken breasts under cold running water, pat dry with a paper towel, and slice horizontally ½ inch thick.
▶ Top each chicken slice with a slice of prosciutto, a slice (or a tablespoon) of cheese, and a sprinkling of chives. Season with black pepper to taste. Roll up and place in a dark 2-quart casserole. You may need to secure with toothpicks.
▶ Cover and bake in the solar cooker for an hour. Bring inside and drain off the liquid.
▶ Whisk together the mustard, wine, and cream, seasoning to taste with salt and black pepper. Pour over the chicken breasts.
▶ Bake uncovered for another hour in the solar cooker, until the sauce is bubbly.

turkey and stuffing casserole

If you live in a part of the country where you can solar cook in November and December, try this easy dish in place of the traditional turkey and trimmings. You can also make it with chicken, and of course, you can eat it anytime of the year. Garnish with cranberry sauce and serve with Baked Yams with Apples (page 122) and a green salad.

YIELD: 4 servings

½ cup chopped onion

5 tablespoons butter

3 cups diced English muffins

¼ cup walnut pieces or pecan pieces

½ teaspoon salt

½ teaspoon poultry seasoning

¾ teaspoon dried thyme

1 (10½-ounce) can cream of chicken soup

¼ cup evaporated milk or plain creamy soy milk

¼ cup chopped fresh parsley

3 cups cooked and shredded turkey or chicken (see page 56)

Store-bought cranberry sauce for garnish

▶ To make the dressing, warm the butter in a large skillet on the stove over medium heat. Add the onion and sauté until soft. Add the English muffins, walnuts, salt, ¼ teaspoon poultry seasoning, and ¼ teaspoon thyme, and toss thoroughly. Remove from heat.

▶ In a bowl, whisk together the soup, milk, ¼ teaspoon poultry seasoning, ½ teaspoon thyme, and parsley.

▶ Put the dressing in the bottom of a dark greased 2-quart casserole. Spread the turkey or chicken over the dressing. Pour the soup mixture evenly over the top.

▶ Cover and bake for 1 to 2 hours in the solar cooker, until the sauce is bubbly.

▶ Garnish with cranberry sauce.

hearty chicken 'n' bean stew

Garnish with grated Parmesan cheese or crumbled feta and serve with Brown Rice (page 84) or pita bread and a green salad.

YIELD: 4 servings

1 (15-ounce) can navy beans, drained and rinsed

1 (15-ounce) can diced tomatoes, with liquid

2 cups whole peeled baby carrots

1 small green bell pepper, seeded and diced

⅓ cup pitted kalamata olives

1 pound boneless and skinless chicken breasts or thighs, cut into small chunks

2 tablespoons olive oil

1 (6-ounce) can tomato paste

¼ cup dry white wine

¾ cup vegetable broth or chicken broth

1 clove garlic, pressed

1 tablespoon minced fresh basil or 1 teaspoon dried

1 teaspoon fresh thyme or ¼ teaspoon dried

1 teaspoon minced fresh oregano or ¼ teaspoon dried

½ teaspoon salt

⅛ teaspoon black pepper

⅛ teaspoon cayenne

1 bay leaf

Grated Parmesan cheese or crumbled feta cheese for garnish

► Place the beans, tomatoes, carrots, bell pepper, olives, and chicken chunks in a dark 2-quart casserole.

► To make the sauce, whisk together the oil, tomato paste, wine, and broth. Mix in the garlic, basil, thyme, oregano, salt, pepper, cayenne, and bay leaf.

► Pour the sauce into the casserole and mix thoroughly.

► Cover and bake for 3 to 4 hours in the solar cooker, until the carrots are tender and the stew is bubbly.

tandoori chicken

A solar oven makes a good substitute for the wood-fired brick oven in which a tandoori dish is traditionally cooked. The secret of a great tandoori chicken is to marinate it overnight. Serve over Couscous (page 89) and accompany with sliced tomatoes and cucumbers garnished with plain yogurt and a little mint.

YIELD: 4 servings

1 medium onion, diced

1 clove garlic

2 tablespoons canola oil or flaxseed oil

2 tablespoons lemon juice

1 tablespoon minced, peeled fresh ginger or ¾ teaspoon ground ginger

1 teaspoon salt

1 teaspoon ground coriander

½ teaspoon ground cumin

½ teaspoon ground turmeric

¼ teaspoon ground cardamom

¼ teaspoon cayenne

¼ cup plain yogurt

4 boneless and skinless chicken breast halves (1½ to 2 pounds total), cut into large chunks

▶ Place all the ingredients except the chicken in a blender. Blend until pureed.

▶ Pour the mixture into a shallow pan. Add the chicken breasts and turn in the mixture to coat thoroughly. Cover and refrigerate overnight.

▶ Scrape the marinade off the chicken breasts and place them in a dark baking pan, reserving the marinade.

▶ Cover and bake the chicken for an hour in the solar cooker. Bring inside and drain off the liquid.

▶ Pour the marinade over the chicken and bake covered for another hour in the solar cooker, until steaming hot.

moroccan chicken and vegetables

Accompany this dish with a fruit salad sprinkled with ground cardamom.

YIELD: 4 servings

2 tablespoons olive oil

1 tablespoon minced garlic

1 small onion, sliced in ½-inch crescents

½ teaspoon ground cumin

1 tablespoon grated fresh ginger or 1 teaspoon ground ginger

½ teaspoon ground turmeric

½ teaspoon salt

1 cup chicken broth

1 pound boneless and skinless chicken breasts or thighs, cut into small chunks

1 small zucchini, cut in half lengthwise and cut into ½-inch-thick slices

1 rib celery, cut into ½-inch-thick slices

1 carrot, cut into ½-inch-thick slices

1 small green bell pepper or red bell pepper, seeded and cut into small chunks

1 turnip, sliced in ½-inch crescents

½ cup canned garbanzo beans, drained and rinsed

1⅓ cups couscous

Plain yogurt for garnish

▶ Warm the oil in a large skillet on the stove over medium heat. Add the garlic, onions, cumin, ginger, turmeric, and salt and sauté until garlic and onions are soft. Add the broth, raise heat to high, and bring it to a boil.

▶ In a dark 2-quart casserole, stir together the chicken, zucchini, celery, carrot, pepper, turnip, and garbanzo beans. Add the broth mixture and stir thoroughly.

▶ Cover and bake for at least 2 hours in the solar cooker, until the carrot is tender.

▶ Drain the liquid from the dish and reserve. Add extra broth if necessary to make 2 cups, bring to a boil on the stove, and add to the couscous. Let sit 15 minutes and fluff with a fork.

▶ Serve the chicken and vegetables on top of the couscous. Garnish with yogurt to serve.

MEATS

BEEF, PORK, AND lamb all do well in a solar cooker, because meat cooked at low temperatures tastes better and is better for you than meat cooked at high temperatures. Have you heard of heterocyclic amines? These are the carcinogenic by-products of frying and grilling red meat. You don't really want to ingest anything like that, do you? Then try cooking your meats with sunshine instead of charcoal.

You can easily adapt your favorite recipes for cooking roast beef, leg of lamb, or pork roast to the solar cooker. Brush the meat with a little oil to seal in the juices and place it in a dark pan with a lid. Add vegetables if you want but wait to season the dish until it comes out of the cooker. Allow about an hour of cooking time per pound and don't worry about overcooking. It's fine to leave meat in the cooker all day—it won't scorch, and it will only get more tender. If you want to make sure your meat is done, use a meat thermometer.

Recipes using ground meat, such as meatloafs and stuffed peppers, also do well in the solar cooker. Some dishes taste better if you brown the meat on the stovetop first, while others come out just fine if you use raw ground meat in the mix.

Soups and stew dishes using meat are also naturals for cooking with sunshine. Just remember that these foods cook more quickly in two smaller containers than in one big one. If you cook in one large pot, it's a good idea to open it and stir once about halfway through the cooking process.

easy pulled pork

This recipe works equally well with turkey, beef, or other lean meats. Serve in sandwiches or over White Rice (page 84) with a green salad on the side. As a variation, omit the onion and cook with ¾ cup barbecue sauce instead of vinaigrette (see Solarcue Chicken, page 67, for a barbecue sauce recipe).

YIELD: 6–8 servings

2 pounds lean pork or other meat, trimmed and cut into 4 to 6 chunks
1 medium onion, minced fine
¾ cup Italian vinaigrette or other vinaigrette

▶ Put the meat in a dark 2-quart roasting pan. Sprinkle the onion on top and pour the dressing over.

▶ Cover and bake for 4 to 6 hours in the solar cooker, until the meat shreds very easily with a fork.

▶ When done, remove about half the liquid from the roaster. Using two forks, shred the meat, mixing with the remaining liquid as you go.

posole

Posole, a Mexican stew, is traditionally made with pork. You can substitute chicken, turkey, or other lean meat for the pork with good results. Posole freezes well. Serve with warmed flour tortillas or over White Rice (see page 84), squeezing a quarter lime onto each serving. Accompany with a green salad.

YIELD: 5–6 servings

1½ pounds pork or other lean meat, boned, trimmed, and cut into 1-inch cubes
1 large or 2 medium onions, finely chopped
5 cloves garlic, minced
1 (29-ounce) can hominy, drained
1 (12-ounce) can diced green chiles
1 pound fresh or 1 (14-ounce) can tomatillos, chopped
1 cup condensed beef consommé plus ⅔ cup water, or 1⅔ cups strong beef broth
1 (6-ounce) can tomato paste
2 tablespoons olive oil
2 tablespoons ground cumin
3 tablespoons chili powder
½ teaspoon cayenne
1 teaspoon dried oregano
½ teaspoon dried thyme
¾ cup fresh cilantro, chopped
2 limes, quartered, for garnish

▶ In one large or two small dark pots, mix pork, onions, garlic, hominy, chiles, tomatillos, beef consommé, tomato paste, and olive oil.
▶ Cover and bake for 2 to 4 hours in the solar cooker, until the meat is very tender. If cooking in one large pot, check for doneness after 2 hours. If more cooking time is needed, stir before returning the pot to the solar cooker.
▶ Remove from the solar cooker and add cumin, chili powder, cayenne, oregano, and thyme, stirring thoroughly. Wait 10 minutes or so for the seasonings to blend.
▶ Stir in chopped cilantro just before serving. Garnish with lime wedges.

cincinnati chili

In Cincinnati, this chili of Greek origin is traditionally made with beef and served over spaghetti. You can make it with turkey to cut down on the fat and serve over White Rice (page 84) if you prefer, since rice can be prepared in the solar cooker more easily than spaghetti. Accompany with Herbed Carrots (page 113) and a green salad.

YIELD: 4 servings

1½ cups water
1 pound ground round or ground turkey
1 large onion, finely chopped
1 (6-ounce) can tomato paste
1 tablespoon chili powder
2 teaspoons apple cider vinegar
1 teaspoon salt
1 teaspoon ground allspice
½ teaspoon ground cinnamon
½ teaspoon ground cumin
½ teaspoon black pepper
½ teaspoon Worcestershire sauce
¼ teaspoon cayenne
1 clove garlic, peeled but whole
2 bay leaves
Grated cheddar cheese for garnish

▶ Put the water in a large dark pot. Crumble the raw (that's right, raw) ground beef into the water. Add the onions, tomato paste, chili powder, vinegar, salt, allspice, cinnamon, cumin, pepper, Worcestershire, cayenne, garlic, and bay leaves.
▶ Cover and simmer all day in the solar cooker, until the meat is tender and the flavors have blended. Remove from the cooker, remove the bay leaves and garlic cloves, and garnish with cheddar cheese after serving over spaghetti or rice.

texas hash

Serve with crusty bread and a green salad.

YIELD: 6 servings

3 tablespoons olive oil

2 cups sliced onions

¾ cup chopped green bell pepper

2 cloves garlic, minced

1 pound ground round or ground turkey

1 (28-ounce) can stewed tomatoes

½ cup uncooked white rice

1 teaspoon salt

½ teaspoon chili powder

¼ cup chopped fresh parsley

▶ Warm the oil in a dark 2-quart baking pan over medium heat on the stove. Add the onions, bell pepper, and garlic and sauté until soft. Add the ground round and brown, separating with a fork.

▶ Remove from heat and stir in the tomatoes, rice, salt, chili powder, and parsley.

▶ Cover and bake for at least 2 hours in the solar cooker, until the rice has absorbed all the liquid and is tender.

bulgur meatloaf

This meatloaf can be made with either ground beef or ground turkey. Try your own favorite meatloaf recipe. And don't be afraid to make a big batch, because leftover meatloaf makes great sandwiches. Accompany with Sweet Potato Salad (page 122) and Baked Cucumbers (page 115) or with Brussels Sprouts Baked with Yams (page 113) and some sliced fresh tomatoes.

YIELD: 6 servings

1 cup bulgur (cracked wheat)

1 cup hot water

1 teaspoon olive oil

2 stalks celery, finely chopped

1 medium onion, finely chopped

1 small red bell pepper, seeded and finely chopped

1 pound ground round or ground turkey

2 eggs, lightly beaten

2 tablespoons chopped fresh parsley

1 teaspoon salt

¼ teaspoon dried sage

¼ teaspoon dried thyme

⅛ teaspoon black pepper

1 cup grated Parmesan cheese

½ cup ketchup

▶ Soak the bulgur in the hot water for at least 15 minutes.

▶ Warm the oil in a medium frying pan on the stove over medium heat. Add the celery, onion, and bell pepper and sauté until soft. Add to the bulgur along with the ground beef, eggs, parsley, salt, sage, thyme, black pepper, and cheese, and mix well.

▶ Shape into a loaf in a dark 2-quart casserole and spread ketchup over the top.

▶ Cover and bake for at least 2 hours in the solar cooker, until the meat is no longer pink.

campfire dinners

Here's an old Girl Scout recipe adapted for the solar cooker. The foil packets make it extra easy to serve and clean up after this meal. Serve with a green salad.

YIELD: 4 servings

1 pound ground round or ground turkey
2 large russet potatoes, peeled and cut into ¼-inch slices
2 carrots, peeled and cut into ¼-inch slices
1 large yellow onion, peeled and cut into ¼-inch slices
4 tablespoons (½ stick) butter
Salt
Black pepper

- ▶ Set out four 12-by-12-inch squares of aluminum foil with the shiny side facing up. Shape the ground beef or turkey into 1-inch meatballs and distribute evenly among the squares.
- ▶ Distribute potatoes, carrots, and onions evenly among the squares.
- ▶ Top each mound of goodies with 1 tablespoon of butter and a dash of salt and pepper.
- ▶ Gather the edges of each square into a little packet and seal. Place in a dark roasting pan, cover, and bake for at least 3 hours in the solar cooker, until the potatoes and carrots are tender.
- ▶ Open the foil packets and turn out onto plates.

burgundy beef stew

You can intensify the flavor of the meat in this stew by marinating it overnight in the wine. The longer you can leave this dish in the cooker, the better it will taste. Serve the stew with Garlic-Dill Buttermilk Biscuits (page 126) or crusty bread, and with a green salad.

YIELD: 4 servings

1½ pounds of bottom round, cut into 1-inch cubes

¼ cup unbleached white flour

2 tablespoons olive oil

2 medium onions, sliced into ½-inch crescents

2 cloves garlic, pressed

1 cup sliced white button mushrooms

2 medium carrots, sliced ½ inch thick

1 cup red wine

½ cup diced tomatoes, fresh or canned

¼ cup chopped fresh parsley

1 teaspoon salt

2 teaspoons chopped fresh thyme or ½ teaspoon dried

1 bay leaf

▶ Shake the beef with the flour in a plastic bag until the meat is thoroughly coated.

▶ Warm the oil in a large frying pan on the stove over medium heat. Add the onions and garlic and sauté until the onions are soft, a couple of minutes. Add the mushrooms and the beef and just barely brown.

▶ In a dark 2-quart casserole, stir together the wine, tomatoes, parsley, salt, thyme, and bay leaf. Stir in the beef and vegetables.

▶ Cover and bake all day, at least 4 hours, in the solar cooker, until the meat is very tender. The longer it bakes, the better.

stuffed peppers

Serve with a green salad and sliced melon, and with French rolls to slurp up the sauce.

YIELD: 4 servings

4 large red or green bell peppers, seeded and cut in half lengthwise
1 pound ground round or ground turkey
2 eggs
½ cup Parmesan cheese
¼ cup seasoned bread crumbs
¼ cup chopped fresh parsley
1 teaspoon minced garlic
1 tablespoon fresh oregano or 1 teaspoon dried
½ teaspoon salt
⅛ teaspoon black pepper
1 (15-ounce) can tomato sauce
½ cup grated mozzarella cheese (optional)

▶ Mix the ground beef, eggs, cheese, bread crumbs, parsley, garlic, oregano, salt, and pepper.
▶ Stuff each bell pepper half with the meat mixture and place in a dark baking pan. Pour the tomato sauce over.
▶ Cover and bake for at least 2 hours in the solar cooker, until the meat is no longer pink. Sprinkle with mozzarella 30 minutes before serving, if you choose, and return to the cooker to melt.

lamb with lentils and rice

The longer you cook this dish, the more tender the lamb becomes. Serve with a green salad.

YIELD: 6 servings

1 pound lean lamb shoulder meat, cut into 1-inch cubes

2 cloves garlic, pressed

2 medium zucchini, cut in half lengthwise and cut into ½-inch slices

2 medium tomatoes, peeled, seeded, and diced

1 tablespoon chopped fresh rosemary or 1 teaspoon dried

1 tablespoon balsamic vinegar

2 tablespoons olive oil

½ teaspoon salt

Black pepper

1 cup dried lentils

1 cup long grain brown rice

2 cups beef broth

1½ cups water

▶ Combine the lamb, garlic, zucchini, tomatoes, rosemary, vinegar, oil, salt, black pepper to taste, lentils, rice, broth, and water in a dark 2-quart roasting pan.

▶ Cover and bake all day in the solar cooker, or until the lentils are tender.

GRAINS

WHOLE GRAINS ARE the building blocks of good health. How handy it is, then, that you can cook any kind of grain in a solar cooker! It's a particularly great method for preparing those grains like rice that don't like to be disturbed during cooking. And for those grains that usually do need stirring, such as grits and oatmeal, the low temperatures seem to eliminate the need to stir. Just combine the grain with water or broth in a dark pan, cover it, and forget about it. Don't worry about leaving it in too long—nothing will scorch. Take it out at mealtime, stir to fluff the grains, and allow to stand for a few minutes before serving—or chill to use later in another dish.

Boxed rice mixes—pilafs, Spanish rice, and such—cook most quickly and easily and are an adequate choice if you're short on time. Simply follow the directions on the package and double or triple the cooking time called for there.

If you have the time and want to exercise more creativity, you can cook up grains from scratch and use them as the basis for pilafs and cold salads. Bulgur (cracked wheat) and couscous (actually a pasta made of semolina durum wheat flour) are the easiest to cook—in fact, they can simply be covered with boiling water and left to stand, but we like the texture better when they've been cooked gently in the solar cooker for up to an hour. White rice, millet, quinoa, barley, and polenta (cornmeal) are generally pretty easy to cook and take a couple of hours. Brown rice takes longer, 3 hours or so.

Grains should be cooked during the peak hours of the sun, between 10 a.m. and 3 p.m. To speed up the cooking, you can boil the water or broth on your stove or preheat it for an hour in the solar cooker before adding to the grain. Grains develop a nuttier flavor if you sauté them for 5 minutes or so on the stove before adding water and baking.

basic white rice

YIELD: 3 cups

1¾ cups water or broth
1 cup white rice
1 teaspoon butter or olive oil (optional)

▶ In a dark 2-quart pot, bring the water to a boil on the stove or preheat it for an hour in the solar cooker. Stir in the rice and optional butter.
▶ Cover and bake for at least 2 hours in the solar cooker, until all the liquid has been absorbed.
▶ Remove from the cooker and fluff with a fork. Allow to stand for a few minutes before serving.

basic brown rice

YIELD: 3 cups

1 cup brown rice
2 cups water or broth
1 teaspoon butter or olive oil (optional)

▶ Rinse the rice well and drain it.
▶ In a dark 2-quart pot, bring the water to a boil on the stove or preheat it for an hour in the solar cooker. Stir in the rice and optional butter.
▶ Cover and bake for at least 3 hours in the solar cooker, until all the liquid has been absorbed.
▶ Remove from the cooker and fluff with a fork. Allow to stand for a few minutes before serving.

rice pilaf

YIELD: 4 servings

1 tablespoon olive oil

1 cup sliced white button mushrooms

¼ cup finely chopped onions

1 cup white rice or brown rice

1¾ cups water for white rice; 2 cups water for brown rice

½ teaspoon salt

2 tablespoons chopped fresh parsley

▶ Warm the oil in a dark 2-quart pot on the stove over medium heat. Add the mushrooms and onion and sauté until soft.

▶ Add the rice, water, and salt and bring to a boil.

▶ Cover and bake for 2 to 3 hours in the solar cooker, longer for brown rice, until all the liquid has been absorbed.

▶ Remove from the cooker and fluff with a fork. Stir in the parsley and allow to stand for a few minutes before serving.

spanish rice

YIELD: 4 servings

1 tablespoon olive oil

½ cup minced red onion

½ cup minced green bell pepper

½ teaspoon salt

1 cup white rice

½ cup water

½ cup vegetable juice

1 cup finely diced fresh tomatoes

2 tablespoons chopped fresh cilantro

▶ Warm the oil in a dark 2-quart pot on the stove over medium heat. Add the onion and pepper and sauté until soft.

▶ Add the salt, rice, water, and vegetable juice and bring to a boil. Stir in the tomatoes.

▶ Cover and bake for 2 to 3 hours in the solar cooker, until all the liquid has been absorbed.

▶ Remove from the cooker and fluff with a fork. Stir in the cilantro and allow to stand for a few minutes before serving.

lemon rice

YIELD: 4 servings

1¾ cups chicken broth or vegetable broth

1 cup white rice

1 teaspoon butter or olive oil

1 tablespoon lemon zest

2 tablespoons chopped parsley

► In a dark 2-quart pot, bring the broth to a boil on the stove or preheat it for an hour in the solar cooker. Stir in the rice and butter.

► Cover and bake for at least 2 hours in the solar cooker, until all the liquid has been absorbed.

► Remove from the cooker and fluff with a fork. Stir in the lemon zest and parsley and allow to stand for a few minutes before serving.

rosemary rice

YIELD: 4 servings

1 cup short grain brown rice

2 cups chicken broth or vegetable broth

1 teaspoon butter or olive oil

½ teaspoon minced fresh rosemary

► Rinse the rice well and drain it.

► In a dark 2-quart pot, bring the broth to a boil on the stove or preheat it for an hour in the solar cooker. Stir in the rice and butter.

► Cover and bake for at least 3 hours in the solar cooker, until all the liquid has been absorbed. Stir in the rosemary and allow to stand for a few minutes before serving.

confetti rice

YIELD: 4 servings

1¾ cups chicken broth or vegetable broth

1 cup white rice

1 teaspoon butter or olive oil

1 carrot, grated

1 scallion, sliced thin

1 tablespoon minced fresh basil

2 tablespoons minced pimento or red bell pepper

▶ In a dark 2-quart pot, bring the broth to a boil on the stove or preheat it for an hour in the solar cooker. Stir in the rice, butter, carrot, scallion, basil, and pimento.

▶ Cover and bake for at least 2 hours in the solar cooker, until all the liquid has been absorbed.

▶ Remove from the cooker and fluff with a fork. Allow to stand for a few minutes before serving.

dill rice with carrots and feta

YIELD: 4 servings

1 tablespoon olive oil

1 small onion, diced

1 cup carrots, cut into matchsticks

1 cup white rice

1¾ cups water

¼ cup chopped fresh dill or 1 tablespoon dried

1 teaspoon lemon zest

1 cup crumbled feta cheese

2 tablespoons chopped fresh parsley for garnish

▶ Warm the oil in a dark 2-quart pot on the stove over medium heat. Add the onion and sauté until soft.

▶ Add the carrots, rice, and water, stir well, raise heat to high, and bring to a boil.

▶ Cover and bake 2 to 3 hours in the solar cooker, until all the liquid has been absorbed.

▶ Remove from the cooker and fluff with a fork. Stir in the dill, lemon zest, and cheese, and garnish with parsley. Allow to stand for a few minutes before serving.

brown rice salad

YIELD: 4 servings

1 cup short grain brown rice

2½ cups water

1 carrot, grated

4 scallions, sliced

8 ounces firm tofu (not silken)

2 tablespoons canola oil or flaxseed oil

2 tablespoons rice vinegar or cider vinegar

1 teaspoon dried dill

½ teaspoon salt

▶ Rinse the rice well and drain it.

▶ In a dark 2-quart pot, bring 2 cups water to a boil on the stove or preheat it for an hour in the solar cooker. Stir in the rice.

▶ Cover and bake for at least 3 hours in the solar cooker, until all the water has been absorbed.

▶ Cool the rice and mix in the carrot and scallions.

▶ Combine the tofu, ½ cup water, oil, vinegar, dill, and salt in a blender and blend until smooth. Toss this dressing with the rice mixture and chill until serving.

basic couscous

YIELD: 2 cups

1⅓ cups couscous

2 cups water or broth

1 teaspoon butter or olive oil (optional)

▶ Combine the couscous, water, and optional butter in a dark 2-quart pot.

▶ Cover and bake for at least 1 hour in the solar cooker, until all the water has been absorbed.

▶ Remove from the cooker and fluff with a fork. Allow to stand for a few minutes before serving.

couscous salad

YIELD: 4 servings

1⅓ cups whole wheat couscous
2 cups water
1 clove garlic, pressed
2 tablespoons olive oil
1 tablespoon balsamic vinegar
1 tablespoon chopped fresh mint
1 tablespoon chopped fresh cilantro
1 tablespoon chopped fresh chives
½ teaspoon lemon zest or lime zest
Salt
Black pepper
Sliced garden tomatoes for garnish

▶ Place the couscous and water in a dark 2-quart pot.
▶ Cover and bake for at least 1 hour in the solar cooker, until all the water has been absorbed. Allow to cool and fluff with a fork.
▶ Combine the garlic, oil, vinegar, mint, cilantro, chives, zest, and salt and pepper to taste and stir into the cooked couscous.
▶ Garnish with sliced garden tomatoes.

basic bulgur

YIELD: 2½ cups

1 cup bulgur (cracked wheat)
1¾ cups water or broth
1 teaspoon butter or olive oil (optional)

▶ Combine the bulgur, water, and (optional) butter in a dark 2-quart pot.
▶ Cover and bake for at least 1 hour in the solar cooker, until all the liquid has been absorbed.
▶ Remove from the cooker and fluff with a fork. Allow to stand for a few minutes before serving.

tabouli

YIELD: 4 servings

1 cup bulgur
1¾ cups water
½ cup finely chopped parsley
½ cup finely chopped tomatoes
¼ cup finely chopped scallions
¼ cup finely chopped cucumber
1½ teaspoons fresh mint or ½ teaspoon dried
½ teaspoon salt
½ teaspoon black pepper
1 garlic clove, minced or pressed
¼ cup olive oil
2½ tablespoons lemon juice

▶ Combine the bulgur and water in a dark 2-quart pot.
▶ Cover and bake for an hour in the solar cooker. Remove, fluff with a fork, cool, and place in a large bowl.
▶ Add the parsley, tomatoes, scallions, cucumber, mint, salt, pepper, garlic, oil, and lemon juice and mix well. Cover and refrigerate for at least an hour to marinate before serving.

basic barley

YIELD: 2½ cups

1 cup pearl barley
2 cups water or broth
1 teaspoon butter or olive oil (optional)

▶ Rinse the barley in a strainer or wash it in several changes of water until the water is no longer cloudy.
▶ In a dark 2-quart pot, bring the water to a boil on the stove or preheat it for an hour in the solar cooker. Stir in the barley and the (optional) butter.
▶ Cover and bake for at least 2 hours in the solar cooker, until all the liquid has been absorbed.
▶ Remove from the cooker and fluff with a fork. Allow to stand for a few minutes before serving.

barley pilaf

YIELD: 4 servings

1 cup pearl barley
1 tablespoon butter
½ cup sliced white button mushrooms
¼ cup chopped scallions
¼ cup pine nuts
¼ cup chopped fresh parsley
¼ teaspoon salt
¼ teaspoon pepper
2 cups chicken broth or vegetable broth

▶ Rinse the barley in a strainer or wash it in several changes of water until the water is no longer cloudy.

▶ Warm the butter in a medium saucepan over medium heat on the stove. Add the mushrooms and scallions and sauté until soft. Pour into a dark 2-quart casserole, reserving some butter in the pan.

▶ Lightly toast the pine nuts and the barley in the remaining butter, and add to the casserole along with the parsley, salt, and pepper.

▶ In the same saucepan, bring the broth to a boil on the stove. Add to the barley mixture and stir well.

▶ Cover and bake for at least 2 hours in the solar cooker, until all the liquid has been absorbed.

barley almond salad

YIELD: 4 servings

1 cup pearl barley
2 cups water or broth
1 cup finely diced carrots
½ cup slivered almonds
¼ cup chopped fresh parsley
¼ cup olive oil
¼ cup lemon juice
1 teaspoon Dijon mustard
1 clove garlic, minced
¼ teaspoon salt

▶ Rinse the barley in a strainer or wash it in several changes of water until the water is no longer cloudy.
▶ In a dark 2-quart pot, bring the water to a boil on the stove or preheat it for an hour in the solar cooker. Stir in the barley.
▶ Cover and bake for at least 2 hours in the solar cooker, until all the liquid has been absorbed.
▶ Cool the barley and mix in the carrots, almonds, and parsley.
▶ Whisk together the oil, lemon juice, Dijon mustard, garlic, and salt. Toss this dressing with the barley mixture and chill until serving.

basic quinoa

Quinoa (pronounced *KEEN-wa*) was a staple of the Incan diet and is the only grain that's a complete protein, containing all the essential amino acids. It needs to be rinsed well to remove the bitter saponin covering before cooking.

YIELD: 3 cups

1 cup quinoa
2 cups water

▶ Rinse the quinoa in a fine mesh strainer or wash it in several changes of water until the water is no longer cloudy.
▶ Combine the quinoa and water in a dark 2-quart pot.
▶ Cover and bake for up to 1 hour in the solar cooker, until the water has been absorbed, the grain has become transparent, and the spiral-like germ has separated.
▶ Remove from the cooker and fluff with a fork. Allow to stand for a few minutes before serving.

southwestern quinoa salad

YIELD: 4 servings

½ cup quinoa
1 cup water
1 cup frozen corn, thawed
1 cup black beans, canned or cooked from scratch, drained
1 tomato, diced
3 tablespoons minced red onion
½ teaspoon cumin seeds
3 tablespoons lemon juice
3 tablespoons olive oil
3 tablespoons minced fresh cilantro
½ teaspoon salt
Freshly ground black pepper

▶ Rinse the quinoa in a fine mesh strainer or wash it in several changes of water until the water is no longer cloudy.

▶ Combine the quinoa with 1 cup water in a dark 2-quart pot, cover, and bake for up to 1 hour in the solar cooker, until the water has been absorbed, the grain has become transparent, and the spiral-like germ has separated. Fluff with a fork and cool.

▶ In a large serving bowl, stir together the quinoa, corn, black beans, tomato, and onion.

▶ Toast the cumin seeds on the stove for 1 minute, or until they become fragrant.

▶ In a small bowl, whisk together the lemon juice, oil, cilantro, salt, pepper, and cumin seeds.

▶ Pour the dressing over the salad and toss gently to mix.

basic millet

Millet is another highly nutritious grain like quinoa, bland on its own and best when combined with other ingredients.

YIELD: 4 cups

1 cup millet
1¾ cups water

▶ Combine the millet and water in a dark 2-quart pot.
▶ Cover and bake for 1 to 2 hours in the solar cooker, until all the water has been absorbed.
▶ Remove from the cooker and fluff with a fork.

spiced millet and rice

Combining millet with rice gives it a more interesting flavor. Sautéing the grains briefly in a little oil lends a nuttier taste and helps avoid gumminess in the finished product. This can become a main dish if you add a can of black beans or pinto beans and crumbled feta cheese after cooking.

YIELD: 4 servings

½ cup millet
½ cup brown rice
2 tablespoons olive oil
2 cloves garlic, pressed
½ teaspoon ground turmeric
½ teaspoon dried basil
½ teaspoon dried thyme
½ teaspoon ground cumin
½ teaspoon curry powder
2 tablespoons soy sauce or tamari
2¼ cups water

▶ Combine the grains, wash, and drain.
▶ Warm the oil in a dark 2-quart pot on the stove over medium heat. Add the garlic and sauté for 1 minute in oil. Add the millet, rice, turmeric, basil, thyme, cumin, and curry powder and sauté for 10 minutes, stirring to brown. Add the soy sauce and water and bring to a boil.
▶ Cover and bake for about 2 hours in the solar cooker, until all the water has been absorbed.
▶ Remove from the cooker and fluff with a fork. Allow to stand for a few minutes before serving.

basic polenta

Polenta is typically stirred while simmering on the stove, but it can also be cooked undisturbed the solar way. Either way, it thickens after cooking. It can be served before it sets, with a variety of ingredients stirred in, or cut into squares after it sets and eaten plain or topped with vegetables, marinara sauce, or meats prepared in sauce. Use yellow corn grits for best results, or substitute the typically more available yellow cornmeal, which is ground finer.

YIELD: 4 cups

1½ cups yellow corn grits or yellow cornmeal
3½ cups water
1 tablespoon olive oil
½ teaspoon salt

▶ Combine the grits, water, oil, and salt in a dark 2-quart pot.
▶ Cover and bake for 1 to 2 hours in the solar cooker, until slightly thickened.
▶ Remove from the cooker and stir in your choice of ingredients, or pour the polenta into a greased pan and refrigerate to set.

polenta two ways

Here are a couple of variations on Basic Polenta (page 96). Try your own variations and adjust the spices to fit the theme of your meal.

YIELD: 4 servings

Cheddar Polenta:
1 recipe Basic Polenta (page 96)
1 cup grated cheddar cheese
1 tablespoon sour cream
Grated Parmesan cheese

▶ Prepare Basic Polenta.
▶ After you take the polenta out of the cooker, mix in the cheddar cheese, sour cream, and Parmesan cheese to taste. Serve warm.

Mediterranean Polenta:
1 recipe Basic Polenta (page 96)
1 bay leaf
1 teaspoon minced garlic
½ cup sliced dried mushrooms
½ teaspoon dried rosemary
⅓ cup pitted green or black olives or chopped sun-dried tomatoes

▶ Mix the bay leaf, garlic, mushrooms, and rosemary with grits before cooking Basic Polenta. After the polenta has cooked, remove the bay leaf and stir in the olives, reserving some to use as a topping.
▶ Pour the polenta into a greased pan and refrigerate to set. Cut into squares and add topping of your choice.

BEANS

BAKING IS A superior method for preparing dried beans, and baking at the low temperatures afforded by a solar cooker is the best method of all, if you can spare the time. Of course, you can always use canned beans in recipes that call for beans, but dried beans are easier to store and cost less. Dried beans should be soaked in water before they're cooked; this shortens the cooking time and prevents the skins from bursting before the beans are tender. The only exceptions to this injunction are lentils and black-eyed peas.

To prepare dried beans, first sort through them and discard little pebbles and defective beans, and rinse them in a colander. Then put them in a pot and add lukewarm water to 2 inches above the surface of the beans. Let them sit at room temperature overnight, or at least 6 hours. Drain off the soaking water. Although this water may contain vitamins and minerals from the beans, it also contains the hard-to-digest carbohydrates that make beans the musical fruit. Then cover the beans with fresh water to 2 inches above their surface, remembering that they'll expand to 2 or 2½ times their original volume, and they're ready to cook.

If you don't have time to soak the beans overnight, you can use the shortcut method, though the beans won't end up as tender. Sort through the beans and cover them with water as described above, then bring the water to a boil over high heat on the stove. Allow the beans to boil for 2 minutes, remove them from the heat, cover, and allow to sit for 1 hour. Drain off the liquid and cover with fresh water to 2 inches above their surface.

Regardless of how you pretreat the beans, allow plenty of time for them to bake in the solar cooker. You can speed them up by bringing them to a boil on the stove before covering them tightly and putting them in the cooker, but this is optional. You can also turn the cooker to keep the maximum amount of sunlight reaching the cooking pot. Allow 4 to 5 hours to fully cook garbanzos, split peas, pintos, navy beans, red kidney beans, and black beans. Lima beans, lentils, and black-eyed peas take less time.

Add seasonings after the beans are fully cooked.

black beans

YIELD: 4 servings

1 cup dried black beans
3 cloves garlic, minced
3 cups water
½ teaspoon cumin

▶ Cover the beans with water and soak overnight. Drain.
▶ In a dark pot, stir together the soaked beans, garlic, and 3 cups water. Cover and bake for at least 4 to 5 hours in the solar cooker, until the beans mash easily with a spoon against the side of the pot.
▶ Drain and stir in the cumin.

refried beans

YIELD: 4 servings

The easy way:

1 (14-ounce) can refried beans

▶ Open a can of refried beans but leave the lid in place, then pull a dark sock over the top and put the whole can in the solar cooker for at least an hour to warm through.

The harder way:

1 cup dried pinto beans

3 cups water

½ teaspoon cumin

½ teaspoon garlic powder

Salt

Black pepper

Chili powder

Vegetable oil

▶ Cover the beans with water and soak overnight. Drain.

▶ In a dark pot, stir together the soaked beans and 3 cups water. Cover and bake for 4 to 5 hours in the solar cooker, until the beans mash easily with a spoon against the side of the pot.

▶ Drain and save the liquid, then mash the beans and add the liquid back in to reach the consistency you prefer. Add the cumin and garlic powder, and add salt, pepper, chili powder, and vegetable oil to taste.

marinated white beans

Start preparing this dish a couple of days in advance of when you want to serve it, because the beans need lots of time to soak, cook, and marinate.

YIELD: 4 servings

1 cup dried navy beans
3 cups water
⅓ cup olive oil
3 tablespoons lemon juice
1 tablespoon white vinegar
½ cup finely chopped celery
1 tablespoon finely chopped green bell pepper
1 tablespoon chopped fresh parsley
1 teaspoon finely chopped onion
½ teaspoon salt
⅛ teaspoon dried thyme

▶ Cover the beans with water and soak overnight. Drain.

▶ In a dark pot, stir together the soaked beans and 3 cups water. Cover and bake for at least 4 to 5 hours in the solar cooker, until just barely tender. Drain the beans.

▶ To make the marinade, combine the oil, lemon juice, vinegar, celery, bell pepper, parsley, onion, salt, and thyme. Pour the marinade over the beans and marinate for 8 hours or more, stirring occasionally.

savory lentil salad

Lentils don't need to be soaked beforehand like other types of beans do. You can start this on the stove as described here if you want to speed it up, but it's not strictly necessary.

YIELD: 4 servings

1¼ cups dried lentils
1 tablespoon olive oil
½ cup finely diced onion
½ cup finely diced carrot
½ cup finely diced celery
1 clove garlic, minced
2 cups water
1 bay leaf
1 teaspoon dried thyme
3 tablespoons olive oil
1 tablespoon red wine vinegar
¼ teaspoon salt
¼ teaspoon black pepper
¼ cup chopped fresh parsley
1 cup chopped cooked ham or walnut pieces (optional)

► Rinse the lentils, drain, and set aside.
► Warm the oil in a dark 2-quart pot on the stove over medium heat. Add the onion, carrot, celery, and garlic and sauté until slightly softened. Add the lentils and water, raise the heat to high, and bring to a boil.
► Stir in the bay leaf and thyme, cover tightly, and bake for about 2 hours in the solar cooker, until the lentils are tender. Remove and cool.
► To make the dressing, whisk together the oil, vinegar, salt, and pepper. Stir in the parsley. Pour over the cooked lentils and stir gently.
► Add 1 cup chopped cooked ham or walnut pieces if you wish.

baked beans

If you like, you can use dried beans instead of canned. Cover them with water overnight and cook them all day in the solar cooker (see page 98), then drain and add the other ingredients for the last 2 hours of cooking.

YIELD: 4 servings

1 teaspoon olive oil
¼ cup diced onion
1 clove garlic, pressed
2 (15-ounce) cans Great Northern or white kidney beans, rinsed and drained
⅓ cup ketchup
2 tablespoons brown sugar
2 tablespoons molasses
1 tablespoon prepared mustard
Salt
Worcestershire sauce

▶ Warm the oil in a small skillet on the stove over medium heat. Add the onion and garlic and sauté until soft.
▶ In a dark 2-quart casserole, combine the onion, garlic, beans, ketchup, brown sugar, molasses, mustard, and salt and Worcestershire sauce to taste. Mix well.
▶ Cover and bake for at least 2 hours in the solar cooker, until the beans are steaming hot.

hummus with sun-dried tomatoes

Serve with pita bread or crackers.

YIELD: 2 cups

¾ cup dried garbanzo beans
3 cups water
2 tablespoons tahini
2 tablespoons lemon juice
2 tablespoons olive oil
1 clove garlic, coarsely chopped
½ teaspoon salt
Black pepper
2 tablespoons chopped sun-dried tomatoes (see page 25)
2 tablespoons chopped fresh parsley

▶ Cover the beans with water and soak overnight. Drain.
▶ In a dark pot, stir together the soaked beans and 3 cups water. Cover and bake for at least 4 to 5 hours in the solar cooker, until the beans mash easily with a spoon against the side of the pot. Drain the beans and reserve the liquid.
▶ Puree the beans, tahini, lemon juice, oil, garlic, salt, and pepper to taste in a blender until smooth. Add reserved liquid if necessary to reach desired consistency.
▶ Stir in the sun-dried tomatoes and parsley.

hoppin' john

This dish has become a traditional food on New Year's Day in the American South and is said to bring good luck in the coming year. If you live in the Northern Hemisphere, you probably won't be cooking Hoppin' John in your solar cooker on January 1, but we think you'll find this version tasty any time of year. You can use peas that are either precooked (canned, frozen, or precooked dried) or dried. With precooked peas, use white rice and slightly less liquid. With dried peas, use more liquid and slower-cooking brown rice. In either case, you'll use the same seasonings. Serve as a main dish with vegetables or as a side dish with fish or grilled meat.

YIELD: 4–6 servings

To use precooked peas:

1 cup chicken stock

3 cups precooked black-eyed peas

½ cup uncooked white rice

To use dried peas:

1½ cups chicken stock

1⅓ cups dried black-eyed peas

½ cup uncooked brown rice

The seasonings:

1 (8-ounce) ham hock, or diced ham or precooked sausage

1 red bell pepper, seeded and cut into 1-inch pieces

3 small tomatoes, diced, or 1 (14-ounce) can diced tomatoes, drained

1 small onion, finely minced

4 cloves garlic, finely minced

½ cup pitted green olives

2 tablespoons capers, drained

3 anchovy fillets, drained and minced

1 tablespoon dried oregano

1 teaspoon black pepper

1 teaspoon ground allspice

¼ teaspoon cayenne

½ cup scallions, white and green parts, sliced thin

⅓ cup chopped fresh parsley

▶ Combine all the ingredients except the scallions and parsley in a dark pot, stirring well.

▶ Cover and bake for 2 or 3 hours in the solar cooker, adding more liquid as necessary until the peas mash easily with a spoon against the side of the pot.

▶ Before serving, stir in the scallions and parsley, reserving some parsley to sprinkle on top.

VEGGIES

VEGETABLES ARE OUR friends, there's no doubt about it. Five servings a day keep the doctor away. Although some vegetables cook better than others the solar way, almost all can be baked by placing them in a dark pan, covering, and leaving in the solar cooker for greater or lesser amounts of time. You can peel and cut up root vegetables, squash, and eggplant before baking, or bake them whole in their skins. Of course, baking them whole takes longer. We suggest putting ¼ inch of water in the bottom of the pot when cooking some vegetables such as potatoes, but this is optional.

- Root vegetables—beets, carrots, potatoes of all stripes, turnips, parsnips—do especially well in the solar cooker, because baking them at a low temperature preserves their flavor and juices, and it doesn't hurt them to overcook. In fact, the longer you bake potatoes, the better they taste. Leaving them in the cooker all day is fine. The laziest cooks like to bake up a whole batch at once and use them throughout the week for potato salad, hash browns, and scalloped potatoes.
- Winter squash also does well but needs a lot of cooking time.
- Solar cooking is a good method for summer squash and eggplant when you plan to puree them, but these vegetables taste better started on the stove if you're going to make something like ratatouille or eggplant Parmesan.
- You can steam greens (spinach, chard, kale, bok choy, beet greens, mustard greens, turnip greens), but they need to be watched closely so they don't overcook.
- You can also steam vegetables like broccoli, cauliflower, Brussels sprouts, and green beans, but these take a very long time to get tender and lose their bright colors in the process. For this reason, you might want to steam these in the solar cooker only when you plan to combine them in some other dish where color isn't so important, like a quiche or a pesto.

■ Any kind of stuffed vegetable can be baked successfully in the solar cooker. Try stuffing zucchini, eggplant, tomatoes, cucumbers, onions, cabbage, chard, mushrooms, or peppers. The harder-to-cook veggies should be blanched on the stove before stuffing, as should any vegetable filling. Stuffings can contain bread crumbs or cooked rice; chopped cooked fish, meats, or veggies; nuts and grated cheeses; chopped fresh herbs; and even fruits like apples, raisins, and dried apricots. Be creative!

asparagus pesto

Asparagus steams surprisingly well in a solar cooker. Eat it plain or blend it into a pesto like the following. Serve on baked potatoes, tortellini, or bread. This keeps well for up to a week in the refrigerator.

YIELD: about 3 cups

1 bunch asparagus, trimmed
½ cup packed fresh basil, coarsely chopped
2 tablespoons pine nuts
2 cloves garlic, chopped
1 teaspoon salt
¼ teaspoon pepper
¾ to 1 cup olive oil
½ cup grated Parmesan

▶ Place the asparagus in a dark roasting pan with ¼ inch of water in the bottom. Cover and bake in the solar cooker about 1 hour, until tender when tested with a fork. Cool.
▶ Chop the asparagus into 2-inch sections and place in a blender or food processor. Add the basil, pine nuts, garlic, salt, and pepper, and blend. With the machine running, slowly add the oil until the mixture is about the consistency of mayonnaise.
▶ Scrape into a bowl and stir in the Parmesan.

green bean pâté

Green beans lose their bright green color when they're solar baked, but that doesn't matter in this recipe, since they end up pureed beyond recognition anyway. Serve on crackers or fresh vegetables.

YIELD: 3 cups

2 cups green beans, trimmed and cut into 2-inch lengths
1 cup walnuts
8 ounces firm tofu, drained and crumbled
2 tablespoons Bragg Liquid Aminos
1 tablespoon minced onion
1 tablespoon olive oil
⅛ teaspoon black pepper

▶ Place the green beans in a dark roasting pan with ¼ inch of water in the bottom. Cover and bake in the solar cooker for 4 hours or more, until tender when tested with a fork. Cool.

▶ Put the cooked beans, walnuts, tofu, Bragg, onion, oil, and pepper in a blender or food processor. Blend until smooth.

baked beets with their greens

Beets retain their flavor and juices best when baked at a low temperature, so solar cooking is an ideal method for them. Beet greens are mild and can either be steamed in the solar cooker or sauté-braised on the stove. This dish is good both hot and at room temperature.

YIELD: 4 servings

6 medium beets with their greens

The dressing (makes 1½ cups):
1 cup canola oil or flaxseed oil
2 tablespoons apple cider vinegar
2 tablespoons tamari or soy sauce
1 tablespoon honey
¼ cup diced onion
¼ cup white (important—don't use dark) miso (soy paste)
Dash cayenne

▶ Trim the greens from the beets 3 inches from the crown. Leaving any roots intact, wash the beets gently and place in a dark roasting pan with ¼ inch of water. Cover and bake for about 2 hours in the solar cooker, until tender when tested with a fork. Cut the tender stems into ½-inch lengths. Peel the beets, cut into quarters, and slice ¼ inch thick.

▶ Strip the greens from their stems, wash very thoroughly, and cut into 2-inch strips. Note that cooking will reduce them to about an eighth of their original volume. You can either place them in the roasting pan on top of the beets for 30 minutes to steam them, or you can sauté-braise them on the stove, first sautéing them in a little bit of olive oil until they start to wilt and then adding a tablespoon or so of water and covering them to steam until tender.

▶ Combine all the dressing ingredients in a blender and blend 2 minutes on high speed.

▶ To serve, lay down a bed of greens, top with the sliced stems and beets, and drizzle with dressing to taste. Use any remaining dressing on green salads or steamed veggies.

beet and potato salad

You may want to bake the beets and potatoes for this salad the day before, since the potatoes take such a long time to cook fully.

YIELD: 4 servings

3 large potatoes
2 medium beets
¼ cup chopped fresh parsley
2 scallions, sliced

The dressing (makes 1½ cups):
1 cup canola oil or flaxseed oil
2 tablespoons apple cider vinegar
2 tablespoons tamari or soy sauce
1 tablespoon honey
¼ cup diced onion
¼ cup white (important—don't use dark) miso (soy paste)
Dash cayenne

▶ Place the potatoes in a dark roasting pan with ¼ inch of water.
▶ Trim the greens from the beets an inch from the crown and leave any roots intact. Place the beets alongside or on top of the potatoes in the roaster.
▶ Cover and bake for at least 2 hours in the solar cooker, removing the beets when tender and continuing to bake the potatoes until tender also, which may be 4 to 6 hours.
▶ Cool the beets and potatoes, peel, and dice into ½-inch cubes.
▶ Combine all the dressing ingredients in a blender and blend 2 minutes on high speed.
▶ In a large bowl, toss the beets and potatoes with the parsley, scallions, and dressing to taste. Use any remaining dressing on green salads or steamed veggies.

brussels sprouts baked with yams

A lot of people don't like Brussels sprouts, but try this flavorful recipe before you give up on them.

YIELD: 4 servings

2 tablespoons (¼ stick) butter
3 tablespoons maple syrup
2 medium yams, peeled and cut into ½-inch slices
¾ pound Brussels sprouts, trimmed and sliced thin
⅓ cup chopped pecans
Salt
Black pepper

► Cut butter into small pieces and melt along with the maple syrup in a dark roasting pan in the solar cooker. Mix together well.
► Place the yams, Brussels sprouts, pecans, and salt and pepper to taste in the pan and toss well to coat with the butter and maple syrup mixture.
► Cover and bake for 2 or 3 hours in the solar cooker, until the Brussels sprouts are tender when tested with a fork.

herbed carrots

YIELD: 4 servings

4 large carrots, peeled and sliced diagonally ½ inch thick
1 tablespoon butter, melted
1 tablespoon fresh chopped dill or chives, or 1 teaspoon dried
Salt
Black pepper

► Place the carrots in a dark roasting pan with ¼ inch of water in the bottom.
► Cover and bake for 2 to 3 hours in the solar cooker, until the carrots are tender when tested with a fork.
► Drain and roll the warm carrots in the butter and herbs. Sprinkle with salt and pepper to taste.

carrots baked with five spices

YIELD: 4 servings

1 tablespoon butter
½ cinnamon stick
¼ teaspoon ground cumin
¼ teaspoon ground ginger
⅛ teaspoon ground coriander
Dash cayenne
4 large carrots, peeled, and sliced diagonally ½ inch thick
1 teaspoon honey
1 teaspoon lemon juice
Chopped fresh parsley for garnish

▶ Cut butter into small pieces and melt in a dark roasting pan in the solar cooker. Add the cinnamon, cumin, ginger, coriander, and cayenne and mix well. Add the carrots and mix well. Drizzle with honey and lemon juice.
▶ Cover and bake for 2 to 3 hours in the solar cooker, until the carrots are tender when tested with a fork.
▶ Garnish with parsley.

corn on the cob

Corn can be baked with or without the husk. Try it both ways and see which way you like better.

YIELD: 4 servings

4 to 8 ears of corn

▶ Trim the tassel end off 4 to 8 ears of corn (depending on your appetite).
▶ If you husk the ears, place them in a dark roasting pan and cover, or place each ear in a dark sock. If you leave the ears in their husks, place them on a dark cookie sheet and cover them with a dark cloth.
▶ Prop the lid of the cooker open slightly to let steam escape.
▶ Bake for 1 to 2 hours in the solar cooker, until the ears are steaming hot.

corn pudding

YIELD: 6 servings

1 (15-ounce) can corn kernels, drained, or 2 cups fresh or frozen corn kernels

1 (15-ounce) can creamed corn

1 (8½ ounce) package corn muffin mix

1 egg

4 tablespoons (½ stick) butter

¼ cup sour cream

▶ Stir together the corn kernels, creamed corn, muffin mix, egg, butter, and sour cream, and pour into a dark 2-quart casserole.

▶ Cover and bake for 2 to 3 hours in the solar cooker, until firmly set. Remove the cover the last 30 minutes to brown.

baked cucumbers

YIELD: 4 servings

2 large cucumbers, peeled and cut lengthwise into ½-inch-thick slices

¼ cup mayonnaise

½ cup instant mashed potato flakes

Butter

Paprika

▶ Spread mayonnaise onto cucumbers and roll in potato flakes. Lay on a dark cookie sheet.

▶ Dot each slice with butter and sprinkle with paprika. Cover and bake for at least 2 hours in the solar cooker, until the cucumber is tender when tested with a fork.

eggplant-tahini spread

Serve on pita bread, garnished with chopped tomato, cucumber, and feta cheese.

YIELD: 2 cups

1 large eggplant, peeled and cut into large cubes

3 tablespoons lemon juice

3 tablespoons tahini

2 tablespoons olive oil

3 cloves garlic, chopped

1 teaspoon dried dill

1 teaspoon ground cumin

1 teaspoon salt

¼ cup chopped fresh parsley

Chopped tomato for garnish

Sliced cucumber for garnish

Feta cheese for garnish

▶ Place the eggplant in a dark roasting pan with ¼ inch of water in the bottom, cover, and bake for at least 3 hours in the solar cooker, until tender.

▶ Drain and cool the eggplant. Put it in a blender with the lemon juice, tahini, oil, garlic, dill, cumin, and salt. Blend until smooth.

▶ Pour into a bowl and stir in the parsley.

▶ Garnish with tomato, cucumber, and feta cheese.

stuffed portobellos

YIELD: 4 servings

4 portobello mushrooms
2 tablespoons olive oil
¼ cup minced onion
2 tablespoons minced fresh parsley
2 tablespoons minced prosciutto
2 tablespoons Parmesan cheese

▶ Gently wipe the mushroom caps clean with a paper towel or mushroom brush. Trim off the stems and mince them.

▶ Warm the oil in a medium frying pan over medium heat on the stove. Add the stems and onion and sauté until browned.

▶ Place the portobellos gill side up on a dark baking sheet. Evenly distribute the sautéed stems and onions, parsley, prosciutto, and cheese on top of the mushrooms, and drizzle with any oil remaining in the sauté pan.

▶ Bake for at least an hour in the solar cooker, until tender and juicy.

parsnips baked with red onion

If you're not a fan of parsnips, which look like big fat white carrots and taste similar, this easy and flavorful recipe will win you over.

YIELD: 4 servings

4 large parsnips (about 2 pounds total), peeled
1 large red onion, sliced thin
2 tablespoons olive oil
2 tablespoons balsamic vinegar
1 tablespoon lightly packed brown sugar
2 teaspoons chopped fresh rosemary or ½ teaspoon dried
½ teaspoon salt
¼ teaspoon black pepper

▶ Slice the parsnips ½ inch thick, then cut the larger slices into pieces about the same size as the slices from the narrow end. Place in a dark roasting pan.

▶ Add the onion, oil, vinegar, brown sugar, rosemary, salt, and pepper and toss thoroughly.

▶ Cover and bake for at least 2 hours in the solar cooker, until the parsnips are tender when tested with a fork.

baked potatoes

It's easy and efficient to bake a batch of potatoes in the solar cooker to have on hand for potato salad, hash browns, and other recipes that call for precooked potatoes.

YIELD: 4 servings

4 large Russet potatoes

▶ Scrub the skin of the potatoes and place in a dark roasting pan with ¼ inch of water in the bottom.
▶ Cover and bake all day in the solar cooker, until tender when tested with a fork.

parsley potatoes

YIELD: 4 servings

4 large red or yellow potatoes
2 tablespoons (¼ stick) butter, melted
¼ cup chopped fresh parsley
2 tablespoons bread crumbs
Seasoned salt

▶ Scrub the skin of the potatoes and place in a dark roasting pan with ¼ inch of water in the bottom.
▶ Cover and bake all day in the solar cooker, until tender when tested with a fork.
▶ Cut into 1-inch cubes and mix with the butter, parsley, bread crumbs, and seasoned salt to taste.

twice-baked potatoes

YIELD: 4 servings

4 large Russet potatoes, baked ahead (see page 118)

⅓ cup plain yogurt or plain creamy soy milk

2 tablespoons chopped fresh parsley

¼ cup grated cheddar cheese

Seasoned salt

¼ cup diced tomatoes or other veggies

▶ Cut baked potatoes in half lengthwise and scoop out the centers, reserving the skins intact. Mash the potato innards with the yogurt, parsley, cheese, seasoned salt to taste, and diced tomatoes or whatever else you have on hand. Spoon the result back into the potato shells.

▶ Bake again for an hour or so in the solar cooker, until heated through.

scalloped potatoes

You can use soy-based bacon or ham substitutes in this recipe if you prefer, or try thinly sliced carrots or zucchini, steamed until tender, for that layer instead.

YIELD: 4 servings

2 large baking potatoes, baked ahead (see page 118) and sliced ⅛ inch thick

2 tablespoons unbleached white flour

½ cup julienned ham, turkey ham, or Canadian bacon

1 medium onion, thinly sliced into rings

½ cup evaporated milk or plain creamy soy milk

½ cup grated Parmesan cheese or cheddar cheese

Salt

Black pepper

Paprika

▶ In an oiled dark 2-quart casserole, place half the potato slices in a single layer. Sprinkle with 1 tablespoon flour. Sprinkle on the ham and onion. Sprinkle with 1 tablespoon flour. Place the rest of the potato slices on top.

▶ Top with the cheese and pour on the milk. Season with salt, pepper, and paprika to taste.

▶ Cover and bake for 2 or 3 hours in the solar cooker, until bubbly.

aunt helen's potato salad

Bake the potatoes for this salad the day before so that you can give them plenty of time in the solar cooker.

YIELD: 6 servings

4 pounds white or red potatoes, baked (see page 118) and cooled
2 eggs, hard-boiled (see page 22)
1 small red bell pepper, seeded and finely minced
1 dill pickle, finely minced
3 scallions, thinly sliced
1 teaspoon sweet pickle relish
1 cup mayonnaise
¼ cup prepared mustard
2 tablespoons dill pickle juice
Salt
Black pepper

▶ Peel the potatoes and cut into bite-sized cubes, place in a large bowl. Peel the hard-boiled eggs and grate them into the bowl. Mix in the bell pepper, pickle, scallions, and relish.

▶ In a separate bowl, mix together the mayonnaise, mustard, and pickle juice. Combine with the other ingredients in the big bowl. Season with salt and pepper to taste.

sesame spinach

This can be served hot or chilled. You can also substitute asparagus for the spinach in this recipe.

YIELD: 4 servings

1 bunch fresh spinach, washed well, stems removed
3 tablespoons prepared Asian-style marinade or Asian-style dressing
1 teaspoon sesame seeds

▶ Place the spinach in a dark roasting pan and add ¼ inch of water to the bottom. Cover and bake for an hour or more in the solar cooker, until wilted and tender.

▶ Drain the spinach and place on plates. Drizzle with Asian-style marinade and sprinkle with sesame seeds.

baked acorn squash

This method works well for any winter squash.

YIELD: 4 servings

2 acorn squash
2 tablespoons (¼ stick) butter
Salt
Black pepper

- ▶ Halve squashes across the midsection and scoop out the seeds and stringy stuff.
- ▶ Cut a small slice off the bottom of each half so that it will sit level. Spread the cut surfaces with butter and sprinkle with salt and pepper to taste.
- ▶ Arrange in a dark roasting pan with ¼ inch of water in the bottom. Cover and bake for at least 4 hours in the solar cooker, until the squash flesh is soft when tested with a fork.

patty pan puree

YIELD: 4 servings

8 medium patty pan squash, scrubbed and roughly chopped
Butter
Seasoned salt

- ▶ Place the squash in a dark roasting pan.
- ▶ Cover and bake for at least 2 hours in the solar cooker, until soft when tested with a fork.
- ▶ Mash with a fork and top with a pat of butter and a sprinkle of seasoned salt.

sweet potato salad

Sweet potatoes take a little less time to bake than regular potatoes. You can just serve them in their skins with a dollop of plain yogurt or make them into a sweet potato salad.

YIELD: 4 servings

4 medium yellow or red potatoes
4 medium sweet potatoes
½ cup mayonnaise
3 tablespoons mango chutney
2 teaspoons curry powder
3 scallions, thinly sliced

▶ Place the yellow potatoes and the sweet potatoes in a dark roasting pan with ¼ inch of water in the bottom. Cover and bake for at least 3 hours between 10 a.m. and 3 p.m. in the solar cooker. Check their doneness with a fork and remove the sweet potatoes when they're soft, since they take less time to cook than the yellow potatoes. Continue cooking until the yellow potatoes are soft.
▶ Cool and peel the potatoes and slice into bite-sized chunks.
▶ Mix the mayonnaise, mango chutney, curry powder, and scallions. Pour over the potato chunks in a large bowl and toss until thoroughly coated.

baked yams with apples

YIELD: 4 servings

2 tablespoons (¼ stick) butter
4 medium yams, peeled, and cut into ½-inch-thick slices
2 apples, peeled, cored, and cut into 8 wedges
2 tablespoons maple syrup
Ground nutmeg
2 tablespoons chopped pecans

▶ Cut 1 tablespoon butter into small pieces and melt in a dark roasting pan in the solar cooker.
▶ Put a layer of yams on the bottom of the pan. Place the apples on top of the yams.
▶ Drizzle the maple syrup over all. Sprinkle with the ground nutmeg and then the chopped pecans. Dot with the remaining 1 tablespoon butter.
▶ Cover and bake for about 2 hours in the solar cooker, until the yams are tender when tested with a fork.

baked tomatoes

YIELD: 4 servings

4 large tomatoes
2 teaspoons butter
Seasoned salt
2 tablespoons bread crumbs
1 teaspoon chopped fresh basil

▶ Core and cut tomatoes in half horizontally. Place in a dark roasting pan. Top each with ½ teaspoon butter, a sprinkle of seasoned salt, ½ tablespoon bread crumbs, and ¼ teaspoon basil.

▶ Cover and bake for at least 2 hours in the solar cooker, until soft when tested with a fork.

BREADS

YOU CAN BAKE just about any kind of bread in a solar cooker—quick breads, yeast breads, fruit breads, biscuits, and muffins—as long as you bake on a clear day during the hours of peak sun (10 a.m. to 3 p.m.). Bread bakes more quickly if it's covered, because steam from uncovered bread will fog up your box cooker window or oven bag and cut down on the sun's rays reaching the bread. Be sure to oil whatever you use as a lid for your pan so the bread won't stick. You can remove the lid during the last half hour of baking to brown the crust.

If you prefer a drier bread and are using a box cooker, you can bake the bread uncovered and prop the lid open slightly to allow steam to escape. If you're using a panel cooker, you can provide a way for steam to escape from the oven bag by closing it with a twist tie wrapped around a sewing bobbin (or other small object with a hole in it). Biscuits and muffins are best cooked this way.

Cooking time for bread in a solar cooker depends on a number of other variables besides steam accumulation—the color of the dough, the size of the loaf pan, the number of loaves you're baking, and the number of times you refocus the cooker. Dark dough bakes faster and more efficiently than light dough if you're baking in a clear pan, so loaves made with all or at least some whole wheat flour are at an advantage over those made with white flour. Small loaves bake faster than large ones, so it's faster to make two small loaves rather than one large loaf. And the more items you load into a box cooker, the more slowly each item bakes.

It goes without saying that dark loaf pans are best at converting sunlight to heat. That said, some dedicated solar cooks have had success baking bread in oiled soup cans or wide-mouthed 2-quart canning jars painted black, and if the batter is dark enough, you can use clear glass because the batter itself will convert light into heat. You can speed up the baking by refocusing your cooker a couple of times to harvest the maximum amount of sunlight.

If a yeast bread bakes too slowly, it may fall and turn out hard and dense. You can set your box cooker out in the sun to preheat for an hour or two before baking to give your bread a head start. On the other hand, if you're starting with frozen bread dough, you can put it in a cold box cooker and let it thaw, rise, and bake as the cooker heats up with the sun. Most panel cookers don't reach temperatures high enough to reliably bake yeast breads, but that doesn't mean you shouldn't try—if your panel cooker has a large reflector and the day is bright and sunny.

Because most solar cookers concentrate heat on the top of the cooking vessel, the top crust may appear to be done long before the loaf is cooked through. One technique that can help is to line the bottom of your loaf pan with waxed paper and turn the loaf out after a couple of hours, then place it back in the pan upside down and continue baking to dry out the bottom. Another technique that may help heat the bottom of the pan is to place a heat ballast such as a brick, a dark tile, or a dark flat rock in your cooker or oven bag, let it preheat for an hour or so, and place your bread pan on top of it.

garlic-dill buttermilk biscuits

YIELD: 8 large wedges

1 cup unbleached white flour

1 cup whole wheat flour

2 teaspoons baking powder

½ teaspoon salt

2 tablespoons canola oil or flaxseed oil

1 cup buttermilk

1 tablespoon chopped fresh dill or 1 teaspoon dried

1 teaspoon minced fresh garlic

▶ In a large bowl, combine the flours, baking powder, and salt. In another bowl, combine the oil, buttermilk, dill, and garlic. Blend the wet into the dry ingredients thoroughly to form a soft dough.

▶ On a floured board or countertop, pat the dough into a circle about 8 inches in diameter. Cut it into 8 wedges and place them separately on a greased dark baking sheet.

▶ Bake uncovered for 1 to 2 hours in the solar cooker, until a toothpick inserted into the center of a biscuit comes out clean.

mexican spoon bread

This custardy wheat-free "bread" is akin to polenta or cornbread. It's a great way to get the superior nutrition of otherwise bland millet into your diet. It can be served topped with a mushroom or tomato sauce, or as a side dish just the way it comes out of the cooker. You can also vary the filling, substituting bits of cooked ham for the chiles, for example.

YIELD: 9 servings

1 cup cooked millet (see page 94)

¼ cup yellow cornmeal

2 cups buttermilk

½ teaspoon baking soda

½ teaspoon salt

2 eggs, beaten

2 tablespoons (¼ stick) butter, melted

1 (4-ounce) can diced green chiles, rinsed and drained

1 cup grated cheddar cheese

▶ In a large bowl, combine the millet, cornmeal, buttermilk, soda, salt, and eggs, and stir until blended.

▶ Cut the butter into small pieces and melt in a dark 8-inch-square baking pan in the solar cooker. Coat the sides well and pour the remaining butter into the batter. Blend well.

▶ Pour half the batter into the pan. Sprinkle with the chiles and two-thirds of the cheese. Then pour the rest of the batter into the pan and sprinkle with the rest of the cheese.

▶ Bake uncovered for 3 to 4 hours in the solar cooker, until firmly set.

▶ Allow to cool and cut into squares to serve.

zucchini nut bread

If you feel like having zucchini nut muffins instead of bread, you can spoon the batter into a dark nonstick muffin tin instead—makes 10 muffins.

YIELD: 1 large loaf

1 cup unbleached white flour
1 cup whole wheat flour
1 teaspoon baking soda
½ teaspoon baking powder
½ teaspoon salt
1 teaspoon ground cinnamon
1 teaspoon ground allspice
¼ teaspoon ground cloves
¼ cup canola oil
¾ cup maple syrup or honey
1 teaspoon vanilla extract
2 eggs
2 cups grated, unpeeled, raw zucchini
¾ cup chopped walnuts

▶ In a large bowl, stir together the flour, baking soda, baking powder, salt, cinnamon, allspice, and cloves.

▶ In another bowl, beat together the oil, maple syrup, vanilla, and eggs, until light. Stir in the zucchini. Add to the dry ingredients and mix well. Fold in the nuts.

▶ Oil the sides of a 9-by-5-by-3-inch loaf pan and place a piece of waxed paper in the bottom. Pour the batter into the loaf pan.

▶ Cover and bake in the solar cooker until a toothpick inserted into the center comes out clean, 2 to 3 hours.

▶ Run a knife around the edge of the pan. Then place a cookie sheet over the pan and invert the pan, allowing the bread to fall out. Immediately peel off the waxed paper. If necessary, continue baking until the bottom is dry.

banana nut bread

If you feel like having banana nut muffins instead of bread, you can spoon the batter into a dark nonstick muffin tin instead—makes 10 muffins.

YIELD: 1 large loaf

1 cup unbleached white flour
1 cup whole wheat flour
¼ cup wheat germ or ground flaxseed
1 teaspoon baking soda
½ teaspoon baking powder
¼ teaspoon salt
¼ cup canola oil
¾ cup maple syrup or honey
2 eggs
3 ripe bananas, mashed
1 cup chopped walnuts

- ▶ In a large bowl, stir together the flour, wheat germ, baking soda, baking powder, and salt.
- ▶ In another bowl, beat together the oil, maple syrup, and eggs. Stir in the bananas. Add to the dry ingredients and mix well. Fold in the nuts.
- ▶ Oil the sides of a dark 9-by-5-by-3-inch loaf pan and place a piece of waxed paper in the bottom. Pour the batter into the loaf pan.
- ▶ Cover and bake in the solar cooker until a toothpick inserted into the center comes out clean, 2 to 3 hours.
- ▶ Run a knife around the edge of the pan. Then place a cookie sheet over the pan and invert the pan, allowing the bread to fall out. Immediately peel off the waxed paper. If necessary, continue baking until the bottom is dry.

apricot nut bread

If you feel like having apricot nut muffins instead of bread, you can spoon the batter into a dark nonstick muffin tin instead—makes 10 muffins. This is good spread with solar-baked Cream Cheese (page 22).

YIELD: 1 large loaf

1 cup unbleached white flour
1 cup whole wheat flour
¼ cup wheat germ or ground flaxseed
1 teaspoon baking soda
½ teaspoon baking powder
¼ teaspoon salt
¼ cup canola oil
¾ cup maple syrup or honey
2 eggs
½ cup plain yogurt
1 cup finely chopped dried apricots
2 teaspoons orange zest
¾ cup chopped walnuts

▶ In a large bowl, stir together the flour, wheat germ, baking soda, baking powder, and salt.

▶ In another bowl, combine the oil, maple syrup, eggs, and yogurt. Stir in the apricots and orange zest. Add to the dry ingredients and mix well. Fold in the nuts.

▶ Oil the sides of a dark 9-by-5-by-3-inch loaf pan and place a piece of waxed paper in the bottom. Turn the batter into the loaf pan.

▶ Cover and bake in the solar cooker until a toothpick inserted into the center comes out clean, 2 to 3 hours.

▶ Run a knife around the edge of the pan. Then place a cookie sheet over the pan and invert the pan, allowing the bread to fall out. Immediately peel off the waxed paper. If necessary, continue baking until the bottom is dry.

buttermilk cornbread

YIELD: 9 squares

1 cup cornmeal

1 cup unbleached white flour

2½ teaspoons baking powder

2 tablespoons maple syrup or honey

⅔ cup buttermilk

⅓ cup melted butter

1 egg

1 cup corn kernels, frozen and thawed or fresh cooked

▶ Stir together the cornmeal, flour, and baking powder. Then stir in the maple syrup, buttermilk, butter, egg, and corn and mix gently.

▶ Pour the batter into a lightly oiled 9-inch-round or 8-inch-square dark baking pan.

▶ Cover and bake in the solar cooker until a toothpick inserted into the center comes out clean, 2 to 3 hours.

▶ Cut into 3-inch squares to serve.

pumpkin bread

Instead of baking in a loaf pan, try using three 10½-ounce soup cans.

YIELD: 1 large loaf or 3 small

1 cup canned pumpkin

¾ cup maple syrup or honey

2 eggs, beaten

¾ cups unbleached white flour

½ cup canola oil or flaxseed oil

1 teaspoon baking soda

½ teaspoon ground cinnamon

½ teaspoon ground cloves

½ teaspoon allspice

½ teaspoon salt

¼ teaspoon baking powder

▶ Stir together all of the ingredients.

▶ Lightly oil the sides of a dark 9-by-5-by-3-inch loaf pan and place a piece of waxed paper in the bottom. Pour the batter into the loaf pan.

▶ Cover and bake in the solar cooker until a toothpick inserted into the center comes out clean, 2 to 3 hours.

▶ Run a knife around the edge of the pan. Then place a cookie sheet over the pan and invert the pan, allowing the bread to fall out. Immediately peel off the waxed paper. If necessary, continue baking until the bottom is dry.

boston brown bread

This bread is traditionally made in a coffee can and steamed, but it bakes just fine in a solar cooker in soup cans. This is good spread with solar-baked Cream Cheese (page 22).

YIELD: 1 large loaf or 2 small

½ cup whole wheat flour
½ cup rye flour
½ cup yellow cornmeal
1 teaspoon baking soda
½ teaspoon salt
1 cup buttermilk
⅓ cup molasses
½ cup raisins

▶ Mix together the whole wheat flour, rye flour, cornmeal, baking soda, and salt in a large bowl. Whisk the buttermilk and molasses together in another bowl and add to the dry ingredients, stirring until evenly moist. Stir in the raisins and pour into a lightly oiled 1-pound coffee can or two lightly oiled 10½-ounce soup cans.
▶ Cover the can or cans tightly with aluminum foil and bake in the solar cooker until firm, 2 hours or so.

onion-dill cheese bread

YIELD: 1 large loaf

2 tablespoons (¼ stick) butter
⅔ cup minced onion
2 eggs
⅔ cup buttermilk
2 cups all-purpose baking mix
1 teaspoon dried dill
1 cup shredded cheddar cheese

▶ Warm the butter in a small frying pan on the stove over medium heat. Add the onion and sauté until translucent.

▶ In a large bowl, beat the eggs and blend in the buttermilk. Stir in the baking mix to moisten and beat about 50 strokes. Stir in the dill, half the onion, and half the cheese.

▶ Lightly oil a dark 9-by-5-by-3-inch loaf pan. Pour the batter into the prepared pan. Sprinkle with the remaining onion and cheese.

▶ Cover and bake in the solar cooker until a toothpick inserted into the center comes out clean, 2 to 3 hours.

egg yeast bread

YIELD: 3 medium loaves

1 packet dry yeast
½ cup warm water
⅓ cup plus 1 tablespoon sugar
2 eggs, beaten
8 tablespoons (1 stick) butter, melted
1 cup warm water
1 cup warm milk
2 teaspoons salt
8 cups unbleached white flour

▶ Put the yeast in ½ cup warm water in a large bowl, add 1 tablespoon sugar, and leave in a warm place for 40 minutes.

▶ Add the eggs, butter, 1 cup warm water, milk, salt, ⅓ cup sugar, and flour and knead. Set in a warm place until the dough has doubled in size.

▶ Lightly oil three dark medium-sized loaf pans. Put the dough into the prepared pans and let it rise again until the pans are two-thirds full.

▶ Cover and bake in the solar cooker until a toothpick inserted into the center comes out clean, 2 to 3 hours.

braided wheat bread

This bread is perfect for solar cooking because it's dark and fits into a round roasting pan. We brought this recipe home from Volunteer Week at the Windstar Foundation in Colorado in 1985.

YIELD: 2 large, round, braided loaves

2 tablespoons dry yeast
¾ cup warm water
1 (12-ounce) can evaporated milk
¾ teaspoon salt
½ cup honey
1½ cups boiling water
7 to 8 cups whole wheat flour
1 cup unbleached white flour

▶ Put the yeast in the warm water in a small bowl and let it activate for 10 minutes.

▶ In a large mixing bowl, whisk together the milk, salt, honey, and boiling water. Add the activated yeast and mix well.

▶ Whisk in, 1 cup at a time, 4 cups whole wheat flour, 1 cup white flour, and 2 more cups of whole wheat flour. Knead in 1½ more cups of flour until the dough is no longer sticky. Then on a well-floured surface, knead in more flour until the dough is smooth and elastic. Let rest 10 minutes, while you butter two dark 10-inch-round baking pans.

▶ Cut the dough in half. Working half at a time, knead for about 5 more minutes and cut into three sections. On a lightly floured surface, roll each section into a snake approximately 18 inches long. Connect the three snakes at the top and braid, then shape the braid into a ring.

▶ Place each braided ring into a pan, cover with a towel, and let rise in a warm place for 30 minutes.

▶ Cover and bake 2 to 3 hours in the solar cooker, until a toothpick inserted into the center comes out clean.

4

what's for dessert?

DID SOMEONE SAY "dessert"? Never has there been a better method than solar cooking when it comes to preparing custards and clafoutis as well as cobblers, crumbles, crisps, crunches, and compotes. Cakes and cookies, pies and puddings can also be baked the solar way, not to mention poached fruit.

The wisdom gained in baking bread with sunshine applies here, especially to cakes. Baking is best done between 10 a.m. and 3 p.m. Dark doughs bake faster than light doughs, and things with crusts come out better if baked uncovered. Prop the lid of your box cooker open slightly to allow steam to escape, or leave a small opening in your oven bag if you're using a panel cooker. Try preheating your box cooker using a heat sink like a brick, tile, or flat dark rock to hold the heat.

A note on the demon ingredient, sugar. (Did you think we were going to say chocolate? Never! Chocolate's health benefits are well established . . . at least by chocoholic scientists.) Despite sugar's evil reputation, some things just taste better with it than without it. If you want to substitute another sweetener such as xylitol, Sucanat, stevia, or organic evaporated cane juice, go right ahead. Where it works, we use maple syrup or honey in these recipes. Using these liquid sweeteners does increase the cooking time, so keep that in mind if you use them as sugar substitutes in other recipes.

deep-dish fruit pie

Almost any kind of fruit can be used in this recipe: apples, apricots, peaches, nectarines, cherries, berries, or any combination thereof. Serve hot or cool.

YIELD: 6 servings

5 cups peeled or rinsed fruit of your choice, sliced ½ inch thick
2 tablespoons honey
2 tablespoons quick-cooking tapioca
1 tablespoon lemon juice
6 tablespoons (¾ stick) butter, in chunks
¼ cup cream cheese (see page 22)
¾ cup unbleached white flour
1 to 2 tablespoons milk

▶ In a dark shallow 2-quart casserole, mix together the fruit, honey, tapioca, and lemon juice.
▶ In a separate bowl, cream the butter and cream cheese together. Add the flour and mix well. Roll out slightly larger than the casserole top between two layers of waxed paper.
▶ Set the pastry on top of the fruit. Fold the pastry under and flush with the rim; flute against the rim. Cut slits to vent the steam and brush with a tablespoon or two of milk.
▶ Bake uncovered for 3 hours or so in the solar cooker, until the crust is done and the fruit is steaming hot.

carrot and zucchini chocolate cake

You don't have to use a dark pan for this cake because the batter itself is dark and will draw and hold the heat. It doesn't hurt if you do use a dark pan, though. The same thing goes for brownies and gingerbread.

YIELD: 12 squares

2 cups unbleached white flour or wheat flour

2 cups sugar

½ cup unsweetened cocoa

1 teaspoon baking powder

1 teaspoon baking soda

1 teaspoon ground cinnamon

½ teaspoon ground nutmeg

½ teaspoon ground allspice

½ teaspoon salt

1½ cups shredded carrots

1½ cups shredded zucchini

1 cup semisweet chocolate baking chips

1 cup canola oil or flaxseed oil

4 large eggs

▶ In a large bowl, mix together the flour, sugar, cocoa, baking powder, baking soda, cinnamon, nutmeg, allspice, and salt. Stir in the carrots, zucchini, and chocolate chips.

▶ In a small bowl, beat the oil and eggs together; add to the dry mixture and stir to moisten well.

▶ Lightly oil a 9-by-13-inch baking pan and spread the batter in the pan.

▶ Bake uncovered for 2 hours or so in the solar cooker, until a toothpick inserted into the center comes out clean.

▶ Let the cake cool and cut into squares.

brownies

These brownies turn out chewy and moist inside, crispy outside. You can melt the butter in a black pan in the solar cooker if you have time. Cut it up into small pieces to speed the process.

YIELD: 9 squares

1 cup lightly packed brown sugar
⅔ cup unbleached white flour
¼ cup unsweetened cocoa
⅛ teaspoon salt
8 tablespoons (1 stick) butter, melted
1 egg, unbeaten
½ teaspoon vanilla extract
½ cup walnut pieces

▶ In a large bowl, mix together the sugar, flour, cocoa, and salt. Beat in the butter, egg, and vanilla. Stir in the walnut pieces.
▶ Lightly oil an 8-inch-square baking pan and spread the batter in the pan. Bake uncovered for an hour or so in the solar cooker, until the top is crispy.
▶ Let the brownies cool and cut into squares.

gingerbread

The crystallized ginger gives this gingerbread a little extra kick.

YIELD: 9 squares

2 cups unbleached white flour or wheat flour
1 teaspoon baking soda
½ teaspoon salt
1 teaspoon ground ginger
1 teaspoon ground cinnamon
1 egg, lightly beaten
½ cup maple syrup
½ cup molasses
½ cup canola oil or flaxseed oil
½ cup plain yogurt
¼ cup crystallized ginger, finely minced

▶ In a large bowl, mix together the flour, baking soda, salt, ginger, and cinnamon.
▶ Add the egg, maple syrup, molasses, and oil, and beat the mixture until smooth and creamy. Then stir in the yogurt and crystallized ginger and mix to distribute well.
▶ Lightly oil an 8-inch-square pan and spread the batter in the pan.
▶ Bake uncovered in the solar cooker until a toothpick inserted into the center comes out clean, about 2 hours.
▶ Let the gingerbread cool and cut into squares.

peach cobbler cake

This is the easiest and most delicious dessert known to humankind. It is in itself a reason to take up solar cooking. Serve with whipped cream or ice cream.

YIELD: 6 servings

3 tablespoons butter
¾ cup unbleached white flour
½ cup brown sugar
1 teaspoon baking powder
½ teaspoon ground cinnamon
½ cup buttermilk
3 cups peeled, chopped peaches

▶ Cut the butter into small pieces and melt it in a dark 9-inch-round cake pan in the solar cooker.
▶ In a large bowl, mix the flour, sugar, baking powder, cinnamon, and buttermilk and beat until smooth. Pour this into the pan with the melted butter. Do not stir.
▶ Pour the chopped peaches into the center of the batter. Do not stir.
▶ Cover and bake for about 2 hours in the solar cooker, until puffed and bubbly.

butternut squash pie

You can cook the squash the day before in the solar cooker. Peel and bake covered in a dark roasting pan with ¼ inch of water in the bottom for a couple of hours or until soft. You can also bake the pie shell(s) in the solar cooker. Place on a dark cookie sheet and cover with a dark cloth; bake for a couple of hours. Serve this pie with vanilla yogurt or ice cream.

YIELD: 1 deep-dish or 2 regular pies

¾ **cup honey or maple syrup**

¼ **teaspoon salt**

¾ **teaspoon ground ginger**

¼ **teaspoon ground cloves**

½ **teaspoon ground cinnamon**

½ **teaspoon ground nutmeg**

3 **eggs**

1 **cup evaporated milk or plain creamy soy milk**

3 **tablespoons dark rum**

2 **cups cooked, pureed butternut squash**

2 **tablespoons crystallized ginger, chopped**

1 **deep-dish pie shell or 2 regular pie shells, prebaked**

▶ In a large bowl, mix the honey, salt, ginger, cloves, cinnamon, and nutmeg.

▶ In another bowl, beat the eggs with the milk and rum. Add the squash and mix thoroughly.

▶ Combine both mixtures and beat well.

▶ Sprinkle the chopped ginger across the bottom of the pie shell(s). Add the filling.

▶ Bake uncovered for 2 hours or so in the solar cooker, until a knife inserted into the center comes out clean. Cool before slicing.

blueberry bread pudding

You can substitute ½ cup dried cranberries for the blueberries in this recipe. Serve with vanilla yogurt or ice cream.

YIELD: 6 to 8 servings

6 cups sourdough bread cubes
2 cups vanilla soy, rice, or almond milk
2 large eggs or 1 tablespoon arrowroot powder
¾ cup maple syrup
¼ teaspoon ground cinnamon
½ teaspoon vanilla extract
1 cup fresh or frozen blueberries, drained
½ cup chopped pecans or walnuts

▶ Butter a dark 2-quart casserole. Place the bread in the prepared casserole, pour milk over the cubes, and set aside for an hour or longer. (Overnight, covered, in the fridge will result in a more custardy pudding.)

▶ Whisk together the egg, maple syrup, cinnamon, and vanilla. Stir this, along with the blueberries and pecans, into the bread mixture.

▶ Cover and bake for about 2 hours in the solar cooker, until puffed and browning around the edges.

egg custard

This is a classic egg custard, usually baked gently in a water bath. Watch the custard carefully to make sure you don't overcook it, or the top will become leathery. Serve with a dab of apricot or raspberry preserves on top, or any other topping of your choice.

YIELD: 8 servings

5 eggs
½ cup sugar
¼ teaspoon salt
3 cups milk
1½ teaspoons vanilla extract
Ground nutmeg

▶ Beat together the eggs, sugar, and salt until lemon-colored.
▶ Gradually beat in the milk and vanilla.
▶ Pour the mixture into 8 dark custard cups. Light cups will work if you put a dark cookie sheet underneath and another one on top. Sprinkle a little nutmeg on top of each.
▶ Bake for 2 to 3 hours in the solar cooker, until a knife inserted into the center comes out clean.

applesauce spice cake

Here's a place to use some of your solar-baked applesauce (see page 26).

YIELD: 9 squares

2 cups unbleached white flour or wheat flour

1 cup lightly packed brown sugar

1 teaspoon baking soda

½ teaspoon ground cinnamon

½ teaspoon ground cloves

½ teaspoon ground nutmeg

1 egg, lightly beaten

1 cup applesauce

½ cup canola oil or flaxseed oil

½ teaspoon vanilla extract

½ cup raisins

► In a large bowl, stir together the flour, brown sugar, baking soda, cinnamon, cloves, and nutmeg.

► In another bowl, beat together the egg, applesauce, oil, and vanilla. Add to the dry mixture and stir to moisten well. Stir in the raisins.

► Lightly oil an 8-inch-square pan and spread the batter in the pan.

► Bake uncovered for about 2 hours in the solar cooker, until a toothpick inserted into the center comes out clean.

► Let the cake cool and cut into squares.

pumpkin tofu pie

You don't need to prebake the crust of this surprisingly delicious (not to mention healthy) pie. Serve with vanilla yogurt or ice cream.

YIELD: 1 deep-dish pie

The crust:
3 dozen ginger snaps
3 tablespoons honey or maple syrup
3 tablespoons tahini
2 tablespoons canola oil

The filling:
1 pound firm tofu
1 (15-ounce) can pumpkin puree
⅔ cup honey
1 teaspoon vanilla extract
½ teaspoon ground cinnamon
½ teaspoon ground nutmeg
¼ teaspoon ground ginger
¼ teaspoon ground cloves

▶ To make the crust, break ginger snaps into a blender and blend to produce 1½ cups fine crumbs, or place in a strong bag and roll fine with a rolling pin. Pour crumbs into a bowl and work in the honey, tahini, and oil until evenly mixed and press into the bottom and up the sides of a dark 9-inch deep-dish pie plate.

▶ To make the filling, drain tofu, crumble, and blend in a blender until smooth. Add the pumpkin, honey, vanilla, cinnamon, nutmeg, ginger, and cloves and blend well. Pour into the unbaked pie crust.

▶ Bake uncovered for at least 2 hours in the solar cooker, until the filling has started to firm up. The filling may still be somewhat soft but will get firmer as it cools.

▶ Chill before cutting.

apricot coconut bars

Some apricot preserves are made without added sugar; that's the kind we like to use in this recipe.

YIELD: 8 bars

8 tablespoons (1 stick) butter, melted
½ cup maple syrup
1 egg
1 teaspoon vanilla extract
1 cup rolled oats
1 cup unbleached white flour
1 cup shredded dried coconut
¼ teaspoon salt
1 cup apricot preserves

▶ Cut the butter into small pieces in a dark 8-inch-square pan and place in the solar cooker to melt.

▶ When the butter has melted, swirl it around the bottom of the pan and then pour it into a small mixing bowl. Add the maple syrup, egg, and vanilla, and beat together.

▶ In a large bowl, stir together the oats, flour, coconut, and salt. Stir the wet mixture into the dry, until well blended.

▶ Spoon half the dough into the buttered pan. Spread evenly with the back of the spoon. With a spatula, gently spread the apricot preserves evenly over the dough. Then use your fingers to crumble the remaining dough evenly on top and smooth it out using the back of the spoon, moistened with water.

▶ Bake uncovered for 2 hours or so in the solar cooker, until the dough is dry and firm.

▶ Cool completely and cut into bars.

poached pears or peaches with raspberry sauce

A simple and delicious use of summer fruit.

YIELD: 4 servings

2 large firm pears or ripe peaches, peeled, halved, and cored
Juice of ½ lemon
¼ cup water
¼ cup raspberry jam or preserves
1 tablespoon white grape juice

▶ Arrange the fruit cut-side down in the bottom of a dark 9-inch-round pan.
▶ Pour the lemon juice over the fruit and add the water to the pan.
▶ Cover and bake for 1 to 2 hours in the solar cooker, until just tender.
▶ Thin the raspberry jam or preserves with the juice and spoon over the poached fruit.

ozark pudding

This comes out as a creamy pudding with the walnuts and apples rising to the top. The apples stay slightly crispy. If you prefer softer apples, you may want to sauté them briefly in some butter on the stove before putting this together. Serve with vanilla yogurt or whipped cream.

YIELD: 6 servings

½ cup unbleached white flour

1 teaspoon baking powder

¼ teaspoon salt

½ cup lightly packed brown sugar

2 eggs

1 teaspoon vanilla extract

2 medium apples, chopped very fine

½ cup chopped walnuts

▶ In a large bowl, stir together the flour, baking powder, salt, and sugar.

▶ In a smaller bowl, beat the eggs thoroughly. Add the vanilla and whisk together.

▶ Add the wet ingredients to the dry and beat into a smooth batter. Stir in the apples and walnuts.

▶ Lightly oil a dark 8-inch-square or 9-inch-round baking pan and pour the mixture into the pan.

▶ Bake uncovered for 3 or 4 hours in the solar cooker, until firm.

▶ Cool before serving.

black cherry clafoutis

A clafoutis is a type of thickened custard traditionally made with black cherries. You could also use plums, strawberries, blueberries, or pears.

YIELD: 6 servings

2 tablespoons (¼ stick) butter
½ cup honey or maple syrup
3 eggs
½ cup evaporated milk or plain creamy soy milk
1 teaspoon vanilla extract
1 cup unbleached white flour
3 cups pitted frozen or fresh cherries
Powdered sugar (optional)

▶ Cut the butter into small pieces in a dark 9-inch-round pan and place in the solar cooker to melt. Swirl to coat the sides.

▶ In a small bowl, whisk together the honey, eggs, milk, and vanilla. Put the flour in a larger bowl, add the liquid ingredients, and mix until smooth.

▶ Pour half the batter into the pan, sprinkle evenly with the cherries, and cover with the rest of the batter.

▶ Bake uncovered for 1 to 2 hours in the solar cooker, until firmly set.

▶ Cool and sprinkle with powdered sugar before serving, if you wish.

fruit crisp

Whether it's called a crisp, a crunch, a crumble, or a cobbler, the idea is the same: top some kind of sliced fruit (apples, apricots, cherries, raspberries, blueberries, peaches, plums, pears, or nectarines) with a crumbly mixture of butter, sugar, flour, and sometimes oats, and bake. Use whatever fruit is in season. Try adapting your own favorite crisp, crunch, crumble, or cobbler recipe to the solar cooker, as well. Serve warm or cool with vanilla yogurt or ice cream.

YIELD: 6 servings

5 cups peeled or rinsed fruit of your choice, coarsely chopped
1 tablespoon honey
1 tablespoon lemon juice
½ cup unbleached white flour
½ cup wheat flour
½ cup rolled oats
⅛ tsp salt
½ teaspoon ground cinnamon
½ cup lightly packed brown sugar
⅓ cup canola oil

▶ Stir together the fruit, honey, and lemon juice. Lightly oil a dark 2-quart casserole and pour in the fruit mixture.

▶ In a medium bowl, mix together the flour, oats, salt, cinnamon, sugar, and oil until an even consistency. Crumble over the fruit.

▶ Bake uncovered for 1 to 2 hours in the solar cooker, until bubbly and browned.

summer fruit compote

Compotes are another healthy dessert dish particularly well suited to the solar cooker and situated to take advantage of the abundance of summer fruits.

YIELD: 6 servings

5 cups peeled or rinsed peaches, apricots, and/or plums, sliced ½ inch thick

1 thin slice lemon or lime, seeded and cut in half

2 tablespoons red wine or water

3 tablespoons honey or maple syrup

⅛ teaspoon ground cinnamon

⅛ teaspoon ground cloves

⅛ teaspoon ground cardamom

▶ Place the fruit in a dark 2-quart casserole. Combine the lemon, wine, honey, cinnamon, cloves, and cardamom in a separate bowl, mix thoroughly, and pour over the fruit.

▶ Cover and bake for 4 hours or more in the solar cooker, until fruit is tender when tested with a fork.

5

menu ideas

YOU CAN MAKE solar-cooked meals as simple or as elaborate as you want to. Because the time of year when solar cooking works best for most people is summer, you may need and want to prepare only one hot dish in the cooker, complemented by a salad with ingredients fresh from the garden or farmers' market, and rounded out with a bread or grain baked ahead of time or in the indoor kitchen. Or you may want to try preparing several dishes at once in the solar cooker. We hope the sample menus for different circumstances that follow will help you start imagining how solar cooking might best fit your particular lifestyle and dietary preferences or restrictions.

ONE-POT MEALS

THERE'S NOTHING QUITE so easy as a one-pot meal. Take one pot out of the solar cooker, assemble a fruit or green salad to get a few more of those essential fruits and veggies, add some rolls or bread from the bakery if you feel like it, and you have a healthy feast.

Tofu Enchiladas (page 42)
Sliced avocados and tomatoes

Lamb with Lentils and Rice (page 82)
Green salad

Vegetable Tofu Pilaf (page 46)
Fruit salad

Stuffed Peppers (page 81)
Sliced melon and French rolls

Crustless Crab Quiche (page 55)
Green salad and sliced fresh tomatoes

Burgundy Beef Stew (page 80)
Green salad and crusty bread

Chicken Mole Tostadas (page 64)
Sliced avocado, cilantro, and sour cream

Campfire Dinners (page 79)
Green salad

Hearty Chicken 'n' Bean Stew
(page 70)
Green salad and pita bread

Posole (page 75)
Green salad and flour tortillas

Texas Hash (page 77)
Green salad and crusty bread

LAST-MINUTE MEALS

IF YOU CAN get in the habit of precooking such ingredients as chicken breasts and bulgur wheat and keeping them on hand in the fridge, you can quickly assemble a satisfying meal on a day when you don't have time to cook. You can also bake nut breads ahead of time, say on the weekend, and keep them unsliced in the fridge until the day you want to use them.

Chicken Salad Véronique (page 57)
Zucchini Nut Bread (page 128)

Curry Chicken Salad (page 59)
Apricot Nut Bread (page 130)

Bulgur Chicken Salad (page 58)
Sliced tomatoes and a green salad

Chinese Chicken Salad (page 60)
Banana Nut Bread (page 129)

EASY MEALS FOR BUSY DAYS

IN ADDITION TO the one-pot and last-minute meals listed above, these meals are easy to put together and can be left in the cooker all day for maximum convenience to the cook. To round out the meal, it helps to have on hand such things as nut breads baked on a day when you have more time.

Artichoke Frittata (page 34)
Banana Nut Bread (page 129)
Fruit salad

Macaroni and Cheese (page 40)
Tuna salad

Stuffed Manicotti (page 39)
Garlic bread
Green salad

Baked Beans (page 103)
Buttermilk Cornbread (page 131)
or Brown Bread (page 133)
Green salad

White Fish with Capers (page 48)
Baked Potatoes (page 118)
Green salad

Cajun Catfish (page 51)
Rice Pilaf (page 85)
Coleslaw

Chicken Divan (page 61)
White Rice (page 84)
Baked Tomatoes (page 123)
Fruit salad

Easy Pulled Pork (page 74)
White Rice (page 84)
Green salad

FANCY MEALS FOR WEEKENDS

THESE ARE MEALS that require a little more attention, either in preparation or in coordinating several different dishes in the solar cooker. Refer to the suggested cooking times in the recipes to get a feeling for which dishes should go in first, and allow more time for cooking several different dishes than each would require by itself. Or put all pots in early in the day, aim the cooker at high noon, and forget about it until dinnertime.

Eggplant Parmesan (page 37)
Garlic-Dill Buttermilk Biscuits
(page 126)
Spinach salad

Veggie Lasagna (page 41)
Garlic bread
Green salad

Stuffed Chard (page 44)
Herbed Carrots (page 113)
Sliced fresh tomatoes

Scallops with Mushrooms and Shallots
(page 54)
Confetti Rice (page 87)
Sesame Spinach (page 120)

Chicken Yogurt Enchilada Casserole
(page 63)
Spanish Rice (page 85)
Refried Beans (page 100)
Shredded cabbage with
ranch dressing and salsa

Margarita Chicken (page 65)
Black Beans (page 99)
Sliced avocado

Chicken Breast Roll-Ups (page 68)
Rosemary Rice (page 86)
Baked Acorn Squash (page 121)
Green salad

Chicken with Sun-Dried Tomatoes
(page 66)
Bulgur (page 89)
Steamed spinach or chard

Tandoori Chicken (page 71)
Couscous (page 88)
Sliced tomatoes and cucumbers
with yogurt and mint

Bulgur Meatloaf (page 78)
Brussels Sprouts Baked with Yams
(page 113)
Sliced fresh tomatoes

Cincinnati Chili (page 76)
White Rice (page 64)
Herbed Carrots (page 113)
Green salad

EASY-TO-COOK MEALS FOR PARTLY CLOUDY DAYS

YOU CAN COOK with sunshine even on a partly cloudy day, as long as the sun peeks through for at least twenty minutes of every hour. But foods will cook more slowly, so you should attempt only easy-to-cook dishes on these days. The following menus include dishes that are most likely to cook thoroughly if you leave them in the cooker all day long as the sun moves in and out.

Chiles Rellenos Casserole (page 30)
Spanish Rice (page 85)
Canned refried beans
Green salad

Crustless Veggie Quiche (page 35)
Tabouli (page 90)
Fresh fruit

Cheese Strata Dijonnaise (page 36)
Southwestern Quinoa Salad (page 93)
Fresh fruit

Pesto Pizza (page 38)
Green salad

Macaroni and Cheese (page 40)
Tuna salad

Stuffed Manicotti (page 39)
Garlic bread
Green salad

Tofu Enchiladas (page 42)
Sliced avocados and tomatoes

cooking with sunshine

Fillet of Sole Amandine (page 52)
Lemon Rice (page 86)
Spinach salad

Poached Salmon with Tomato-Basil
Mayonnaise (page 49)
Lemon Rice (page 86)
Green salad

Teriyaki Salmon (page 50)
White Rice (page 84)
Spinach salad

Shrimp with Prosciutto and Basil
(page 53)
Couscous Salad (page 89)
Sliced fresh tomatoes

Crustless Crab Quiche (page 55)
Green salad and sliced fresh tomatoes

Cajun Catfish (page 51)
Rice Pilaf (page 85)
Coleslaw

Chicken Divan (page 61)
White Rice (page 84)
Baked Tomatoes (page 123)
Fruit salad

Chicken Mole Tostadas (page 64)
Sliced avocado, cilantro, and sour cream

VEGAN MEALS

ALL OF THESE menus are also suitable for low-fat, high-fiber diets.

Coconut-Vegetable Fusion (page 43)
Brown Rice (page 84)
Steamed greens

Southwestern Quinoa Salad (page 93)
Corn tortillas
Sliced avocado

Vegetable Tofu Pilaf (page 46)
Fruit salad

Barley Almond Salad (page 92)
Green Bean Pate (page 110) with rye or
rice crackers
Fresh fruit

Tabouli (page 90)
Eggplant-Tahini Spread (page 116)
Hummus with Sun-Dried Tomatoes
(page 104)
Pita bread

Ratatouille (page 45)
Brown Rice (page 84)
Fresh fruit

Savory Lentil Salad (page 102)
Spiced Millet and Rice (page 85)
Spinach salad

Sweet Potato Salad (page 122)
Sesame Spinach (page 120)
Corn on the Cob (page 114)

Parsnips Baked with Red Onion
(page 117)
Green Bean Pate (page 110)
with rye or rice crackers
Beets Baked with Their Greens
(page 111)

Marinated White Beans (page 101)
Spiced Millet and Rice (page 95)
Sliced fresh tomatoes
Green salad

Spanish Rice (page 85)
Black Beans (page 99)
Corn on the Cob (page 114)

Brown Rice Salad (page 88)
Sesame Spinach (page 120)
Sliced fresh tomatoes

WHEAT-FREE MEALS

Coconut-Vegetable Fusion (page 43)
Brown Rice (page 84)
Steamed greens

Southwestern Quinoa Salad (page 93)
Corn tortillas
Sliced avocado

Barley Almond Salad (page 92)
Green Bean Pate (page 110)
with rye or rice crackers
Fresh fruit

Ratatouille (page 45)
Brown Rice (page 84)
Fresh fruit

Savory Lentil Salad (page 102)
Spiced Millet and Rice (page 95)
Spinach salad

Sweet Potato Salad (page 122)
Sesame Spinach (page 120)
Corn on the Cob (page 114)

Parsnips Baked with Red Onion
(page 117)
Green Bean Pate (page 110)
with rye or rice crackers
Beets Baked with Their Greens
(page 111)

Marinated White Beans (page 101)
Spiced Millet and Rice (page 95)
Sliced fresh tomatoes

Green salad
Tofu Enchiladas (page 42)
Sliced avocados and tomatoes

Spanish Rice (page 85)
Black Beans (page 99)
Corn on the Cob (page 114)

Brown Rice Salad (page 88)
Sesame Spinach (page 120)
Sliced fresh tomatoes

Cajun Catfish (page 51)
Rice Pilaf (page 85)
Coleslaw

Fillet of Sole Amandine (page 52)
Lemon Rice (page 86)
Spinach salad

Poached Salmon with
Tomato-Basil Mayonnaise (page 49)
Lemon Rice (page 86)
Green salad

Teriyaki Salmon (page 50)
White Rice (page 84)
Spinach salad

Chicken Divan (page 61)
White Rice (page 84)
Baked Tomatoes (page 123)
Fruit salad

Tandoori Chicken (page 71)
Couscous (page 88)
Sliced tomatoes and cucumbers with
yogurt and mint

Chicken Mole Tostadas (page 64)
Sliced avocado, cilantro, and sour cream
Margarita Chicken (page 65)
Black Beans (page 99)
Sliced avocado

Chicken Breast Roll-Ups (page 68)
Rosemary Rice (page 86)
Baked Acorn Squash (page 121)
Green salad

Cincinnati Chili (page 76)
White Rice (page 84)
Herbed Carrots (page 113)
Green salad

Easy Pulled Pork (page 74)
White Rice (page 84)
Green salad

Lamb with Lentils and Rice (page 82)
Green salad

Campfire Dinners (page 79)
Green salad

6

building a solar cooker

IN THIS CHAPTER we outline how to build two different solar cookers: a panel cooker and a box cooker. Both types are proven designs, and each has its advantages and shortcomings.

Solar cooks have invented countless variations on these basic designs, so feel free to improvise. For example, a simple box cooker typically has a lid that lifts off to provide access to the interior. A door in the side or back of the box might be more convenient, but it would need to fit snugly and be well insulated to limit heat loss. Designers who have made such doors usually discover that they need to use plywood or other building material instead of cardboard, driving up the cost of the box.

Building a solar cooker according to our instructions is easy once you've gathered the materials. Putting a box cooker together will take several hours—but if you start early in the day, you may be cooking by afternoon. Building a panel cooker is even easier than a box cooker and will take an hour or two after you've gathered the materials. To help you decide which type of cooker you want to build, we'll first give you an overview of each solar cooker and its design.

▶ OVERVIEW OF BOX AND PANEL COOKERS AND THEIR ANATOMY

THE BOX COOKER

The solar box cooker focuses sunlight on a dark cooking pot through a pane of glass or plastic and retains the generated heat within an insulated box. The box cooker presented here is from a design originally patented and popularized by Barbara Kerr.

Box cookers can accommodate several pots at once. They're fairly stable in windy conditions and aren't particularly sensitive to the ambient air temperature, since they're well insulated. They keep foods warm for quite a while after the sun has left the box. They don't need to be turned to follow the sun, unless you're cooking something like beans that takes a particularly long time. They keep pots safely out of reach of small hands that might find out the hard way that black cooking vessels get hot in the sun. On the negative side, they're more difficult to build than a panel cooker and require more storage space.

A box cooker is composed of six major elements:

- A large outer box lined with aluminum foil
- A smaller box that nests inside the outer box and is coated over its entire surface with aluminum foil
- Insulation to stuff in between the boxes
- A glass or plastic film window to cover the top of the nested boxes
- A reflecting lid that when propped open reflects extra sunlight into the cooker and when closed protects the window and helps hold heat in after the sun has gone
- Optionally, a dark-surfaced metal drip pan on the floor of the cooker that catches drips and helps distribute heat

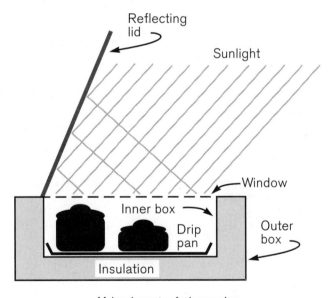

Major elements of a box cooker

THE PANEL COOKER

The solar panel cooker uses a reflective panel to focus sunlight on a dark cooking pot, which is protected from convection and radiation heat loss by a clear plastic oven bag. The design presented here is a variation of the CooKit popularized by Solar Cookers International.

Panel cookers are designed to cook smaller portions, usually in only one pot, but they may cook slightly faster than a box cooker. They can be folded flat for storage and are comparatively cheap and easy to build. They heat food fast and raise its temperature at least as much as a box cooker on a hot sunny day, but since the oven bag required to hold heat around the pot mostly prevents heat loss by convection (not radiation), the panel cooker isn't as good as a box cooker at preserving heat when the sun goes away. You'll need more than one panel cooker if you want to cook multiple dishes at one time. And it's awkward—though not impossible—to bake dishes uncovered in a panel cooker, since the oven bag has a tendency to collapse around the cooking vessel when it gets hot. Panel cookers are also typically less stable than box cookers in windy conditions and need to be turned more often than box cookers to keep the maximum amount of sunlight on the cooking pot, since they have side reflectors that can shade the pot.

A panel cooker is composed of three elements:

- A reflector, which we'll fashion from a large cardboard panel cut to shape, creased and folded, and coated on one side with aluminum foil
- A plastic oven bag or other transparent container to insulate the cooking pot from convection and infrared radiation heat loss
- A wooden block, wire stand, brick, coil of rope, or other small platform to insulate the cooking pot from the panel

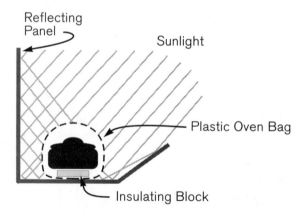

Major elements of a panel cooker

▶ BUILDING A BOX COOKER

BEFORE YOU START to build your solar box cooker, read all of the building instructions. You'll need to make some decisions as you go, and by reading all of the instructions first, you can see how your decisions will affect the final product. Note that the sturdier the cardboard you use, the better. Sturdy boxes can last for years, especially if you protect the outside of the larger box with paint, wax, or contact paper.

GATHER THE MATERIALS

To build your solar box cooker, you'll need these materials and tools:

- A **large cardboard box** to serve as the inside of your cooker. Ideally, this inner box should be just deep enough for your tallest cooking pot, plus an inch or so of headroom. The shallower the box, the less heat will escape through the side walls. A rectangular box is better than a square one. If its front is longer than its side, your oven will be less sensitive to the motion of the sun and won't need to be rotated as frequently. For a pot 7 inches high, a box 8 x 20 x 24 inches (20 x 51 x 61 cm) would be about right.

- An **even larger cardboard box** to serve as the outside of the cooker. The inner box should nest comfortably inside this box, with a clearance of about 2 inches on all sides (although more space is OK). This outer box should also be about 2 inches taller than the inner box. If your inner box measures 8 x 20 x 24 inches (20 x 51 x 61 cm), your outer box should measure about 10 x 24 x 28 (25.5 x 61 x 71 cm). You'll be filling the space between the boxes with insulation.

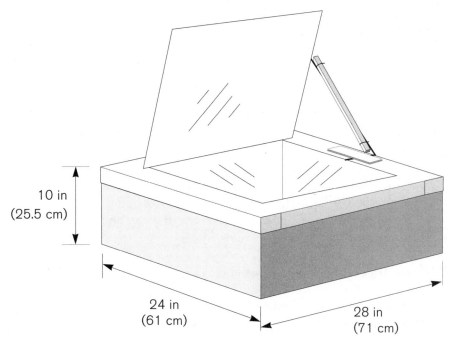

10 in
(25.5 cm)

24 in
(61 cm)

28 in
(71 cm)

Overall dimensions of the ideal solar box cooker

- A **piece of glass or plastic oven bag** at least 20 inches square to cover the top of the nested boxes. If you're using a piece of glass, it should ideally be slightly larger than the inner box and slightly smaller than the outer box. Ordinary window glass works better than plate or safety glass. In cool or windy climates you

building a solar cooker

might want to use a piece of double-pane glass or two pieces of ordinary glass with "dead air" trapped between them. If you have an old window on hand, you can take it to a glass shop to get it cut to a convenient size. If you don't have a piece of glass, a glass shop will sell you one.

As an alternative, you can use a plastic oven bag in place of the glass. Find a large one designed for cooking a turkey. If the doubled bag is big enough, you can seal its open edge (to eliminate condensation buildup) and use it as is; otherwise, you'll need to slit the bag along two edges and use it as a single layer. The bag will eventually turn brittle and crack after exposure to ultraviolet light, so be prepared to replace it after a year or two.

- Enough **aluminum foil** to cover the inside of the larger box and both sides of the smaller box—a small roll is usually enough. Regular thickness foil actually works better than heavy-duty foil because it conducts less heat away from the hot interior of the oven.

- **Insulation** to stuff in between the boxes. Crumpled newspaper works just fine, as does straw, wool fleece, dry grass, or wood shavings. Stay away from Styrofoam or other plastics that might melt or give off toxic gas when heated. If you plan to use newspaper, save up your papers for a week or two—you'll need a good supply. Avoid paper with color printing because it's denser and doesn't insulate as well. If the space between the boxes is less than 2 inches, try slipping in a foil-covered cardboard panel.

- **Additional cardboard**. One piece will serve as a reflecting lid. Although its size isn't critical, it should be large enough to cover the window. You'll need another large piece to use as a window frame on the top of the cooker. You'll also need some small pieces to support the floor of the inner box so that the weight of your cookware doesn't crush the insulation. You may also need extra cardboard to seal the space between the inner and outer boxes at the top of the cooker. And you may want a large piece to serve as a drip pan on the bottom of the inner box.

- A **box-cutting knife or heavy shears** to cut the cardboard and foil.

- A sturdy **straightedge** and **large spoon** or other rounded metal object to score the cardboard before creasing and folding it.

- About 8 ounces of **water-soluble glue** such as Elmer's Glue-All.

- A **small container** in which to mix the glue with water.

- An **old paintbrush** to spread the glue.

- **Caulking or adhesive** to hold the window glass or plastic film to the cardboard lid.

- An 18-inch or so piece of **stiff wire** such as a coat hanger, and a **stick** to prop the reflector open.

- Optionally, a **dark cookie sheet or metal tray** to use as a drip pan. The drip pan must be able to fit inside the smaller box. If you don't have a dark metal tray, you can substitute a foil-covered piece of cardboard and paint the top side with black tempera or other nontoxic black paint.

After you've gathered all the materials, you're ready to start putting your solar box cooker together.

SIZE UP THE BOXES

Put the smaller box inside the larger one and size them up. The inner box should have a clearance of about 2 inches on all four sides. The outer box should be about 2 inches taller than the inner box. If the boxes need trimming, don't cut them yet. First, you need to decide how you'll cover the gap between the top edges of the boxes.

Basically, you have three options for covering the gap. These options are illustrated later in the instructions.

- Option 1: If the outer box has top flaps, you can notch them so that they'll fold down inside the inner box and cover the gap.
- Option 2: If neither box has top flaps, you can make "toppers" out of cardboard to cover the gap.
- Option 3: If the inner box has top flaps, you can use them in combination with either outer box flaps or toppers to cover the gap.

You don't have to worry about the details of covering the top gap just yet. You'll do that in a later step. At this point, just decide which approach you'll take and trim the boxes if you need to so that they're the right size.

If the boxes have top flaps, leave them in place for now. If you need to make either of the boxes smaller, slit them along their corners without cutting off the top flaps. Then, using a long straightedge and a piece of smooth metal like the rounded edge of a large spoon, score a line where you want the top of the box to be and make a fold in each top flap to define the top edge of the box.

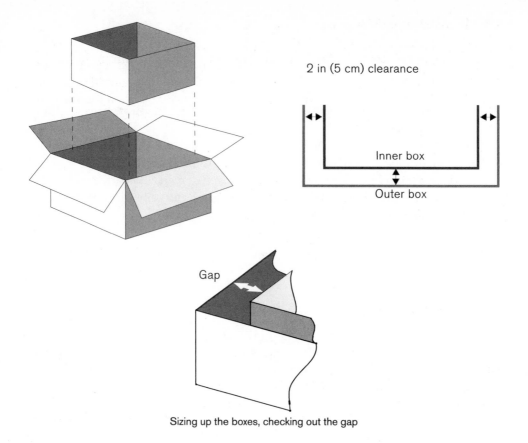

2 in (5 cm) clearance

Inner box

Outer box

Gap

Sizing up the boxes, checking out the gap

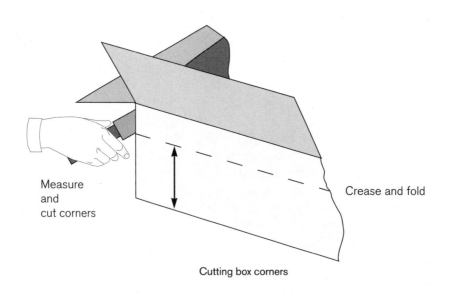

Measure
and
cut corners

Crease and fold

Cutting box corners

GLUE FOIL ON THE BOXES

Mix the glue with about two parts water and brush it onto the inside of the bigger box, including the bottom. If the box has top flaps, ignore them for now. Then cover the glued surface with aluminum foil. Most foil has a shiny side and a dull side—glue the dull side to the box so that the shiny side is exposed. Overlap the seams at least half an inch. No one will see the inside of the larger box, so this is a good place to start while honing your wallpapering skills.

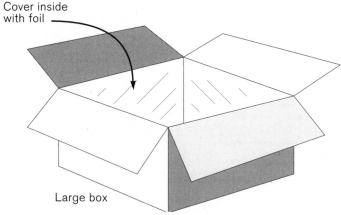

Cover inside with foil

Large box

Gluing foil to the inside of the large box

Do the same thing with the smaller box, but this time cover both the inside and the outside surfaces with foil. Again, ignore the flaps for now.

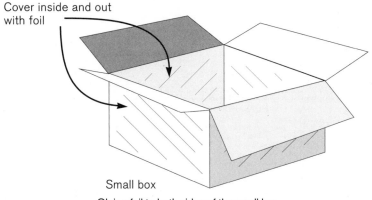

Cover inside and out with foil

Small box

Gluing foil to both sides of the small box

MAKE THE BOTTOM SUPPORTS

While the glue is drying, cut out some cardboard squares 3 or 4 inches on each edge. Make them uniform in size because you'll be stacking them up into little pillars to support the inner box from underneath. You'll need one stack for each corner of the inner box, plus three or four more to support the center. Glue the cardboard squares together into stacks high enough to bring the top of the inner box level with the top of the outer box.

When the glue on the boxes is dry enough so that the foil stays put, place the cardboard stacks in the bottom of the outer box and arrange them to support the floor of the cooker. Check the position and height of the stacks by setting the inner box on them. When you've properly positioned the stacks, glue them in place on the floor of the outer box.

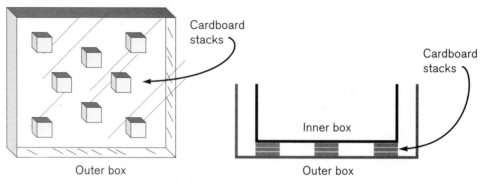

Putting in the bottom supports

ADD THE INSULATION

Crumple newspaper (or gather another kind of insulation) and stuff it into the bottom of the outer box between and to the height of the cardboard stacks. Then place the inner box on top of the insulation and center it in the outer box. Stuff the space between the sides with more insulation.

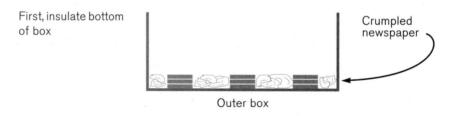

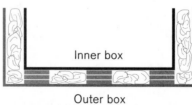

Adding the insulation

cooking with sunshine

COVER THE GAP

Next you'll cover the gap between the top edges of the inner and outer boxes. The result of covering the gap should be an even top surface that will leave no air gaps when mated with a lid you'll make later.

Earlier, you considered three options for covering the gap between the boxes. Now you'll actually do it, using the flaps still on the boxes or separate pieces of cardboard we'll call toppers. You can use a combination of inner and outer box flaps and toppers. The design you wind up with will depend on the boxes you've chosen.

If the outer box has top flaps, you can use these to cover the gap as follows:

- Fold one opposite pair of flaps inward. Cut two notches in each flap so that part of the flap covers the gap and part folds down into the inner box. Before folding the flap, crease it with a spoon or other metal object so that it will bend smoothly.

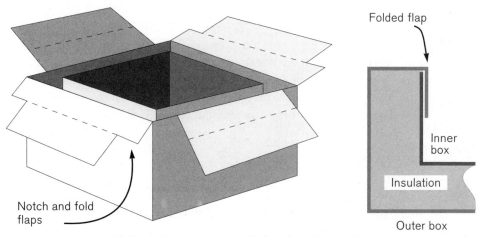

Option 1: Covering the gap with flaps from the outer box

- Notch and fold the opposite pair of flaps the same way and then trim away the excess cardboard from the ends of the flaps where they overlap. Your goal is to wind up with only one layer of cardboard at the corners.
- Coat the flaps with glue and foil, overlapping the existing foil by at least an inch. Tuck the flaps into the inner box.

If neither box has flaps, you'll need to cover the gap with toppers that you've cut out of extra cardboard. Cover the toppers on both sides with glue and foil. You can either tie the corners of the toppers or glue and tape them to hold them in place.

building a solar cooker

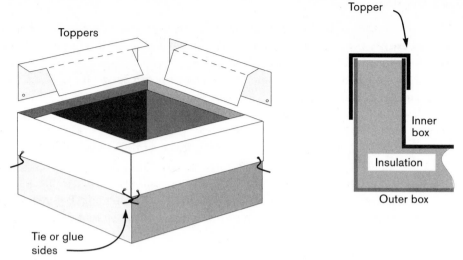

Option 2: Covering the gap with toppers

If the inner box has top flaps, you can use a pair of them in place of a pair of outer box flaps or toppers by folding them over to the outside. In a pinch, you can use all four inner box flaps instead of outer box flaps or toppers, but then you'll need to cover the gaps left at the corners with separate pieces of cardboard and seal the entire gap covering with foil. This isn't a very sturdy arrangement, so use it only as a last resort.

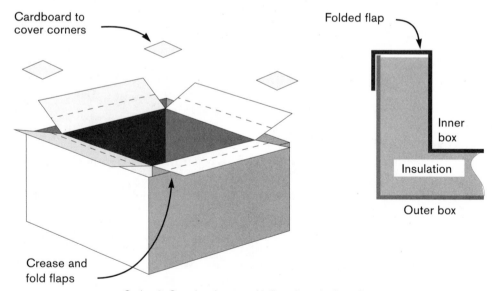

Option 3: Covering the gap with flaps from the inner box

cooking with sunshine

MAKE THE DRIP PAN

A black cookie sheet makes a good drip pan. As an alternative, you can cut a piece of cardboard the same size as the bottom of the inner box and glue foil to one side. Paint this foiled side black with a paint that's nontoxic when dry (check the label to be sure) or with paint you make by mixing three parts water, one part Elmer's glue, and black tempera powder. When it's dry, put this in the bottom of the oven with the black side up.

MAKE THE LID

If your outer box came with a separate lid instead of top flaps, you may be able to make it fit over the box assembly. If your outer box didn't come with a lid, you'll need to make one out of a large piece of cardboard. Get an oversized piece, slit it at the corners, and fold the edges over the outside of the cooker. Secure the corners with tape, staples, or glue.

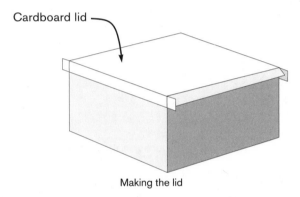

Cardboard lid

Making the lid

Turn your lid upside down and center your glazing (glass or plastic film) on it. Trace a line around the edge of the glazing. Then draw another rectangle about an inch inside the first one. (The adhesive or caulking to hold your window to your lid will go between these lines.) You'll cut along the inner line on either three sides or four sides to make your window, depending on how you decide to make your reflector.

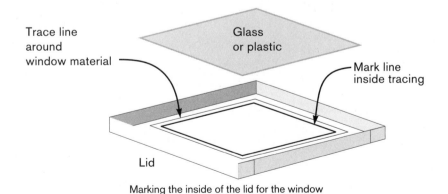

Trace line around window material

Glass or plastic

Mark line inside tracing

Lid

Marking the inside of the lid for the window

building a solar cooker

MAKE THE REFLECTOR

You can make the reflector either from the piece you cut out of the lid along three sides or from a separate piece of cardboard large enough to cover the whole top of the oven. The first way is simplest and requires the least cardboard; the second way is harder and takes more cardboard but protects the window better and reflects more of the sun's rays into your cooker.

To make your reflector the first way, cut along one long and both short sides of the inner line you've drawn on the lid. Fold the flap up along the fourth side to make both the window opening and the reflector. Glue foil to the reflector on the side toward the lid.

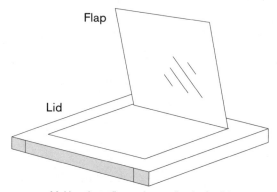

Making the reflector from a flap in the lid

To make your reflector the second way, cut along all four sides of the inner line you've drawn on the lid and remove the piece of cardboard to make the window opening. Then cut another piece of cardboard the same size as the lid. You'll glue this piece to the top of the lid as shown in the following figure, but don't do it until you've installed the window (described below).

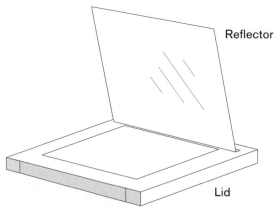

Making the reflector from a separate piece of cardboard

GLUE THE WINDOW TO THE LID

If you've made the smaller reflector, you'll glue the glass or plastic film to the underside of the lid. Squeeze a bead of silicone caulking or adhesive between the two lines you drew earlier on the underside of the lid and lay the glazing on it. If using plastic film, stretch it out smooth and tight.

If you're using glass, you may want to provide it with some additional protection. Apply another bead of adhesive around the edge of the glass and glue on a cardboard frame, making a sandwich of the glass inside the cardboard. If you don't have a piece of cardboard big enough to make a single-piece frame, you can get the same effect with a separate strip along each edge of the glass. You'll want a firm, tight seal here, so weigh down the assembly until the adhesive dries.

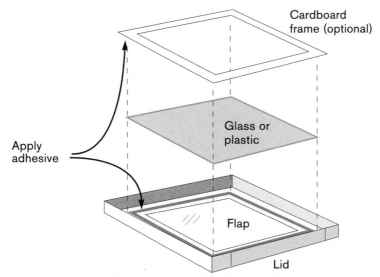

Mounting the window in a lid with a flap reflector

If you've made the larger reflector, you can glue your glazing to either the top or the underside of the lid. If you're using glass, gluing it to the top of the lid may be more secure. If you decide to glue your glazing to the top of the lid, you'll need to glue the hinge of the reflector to the lid at least an inch away from the window opening to allow enough room. If you mount your glazing on the underside of the lid, the placement of the reflector hinge isn't critical.

To glue the glazing to the top of the lid, squeeze a bead of silicone caulking or adhesive around the opening you've cut in the lid and lay the glass or plastic film on it. Allow the caulking or adhesive to dry.

Now crease the piece of cardboard you're going to use as a reflector an inch or so in from one of the long edges. Again using caulking or adhesive, glue this part of the reflector to the lid. When the adhesive has set, coat the side of the reflector that faces the lid with aluminum foil.

building a solar cooker

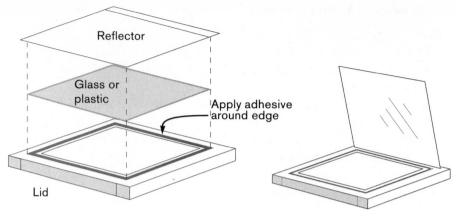

Mounting the window on a lid with a separate reflector

MAKE THE REFLECTOR PROP

You'll need to prop up the reflector to keep it from falling down on top of the window and from blowing backward in the breeze. One easy solution is to use a piece of stiff coat hanger wire and a wooden stick. If your reflector is approximately the width of the

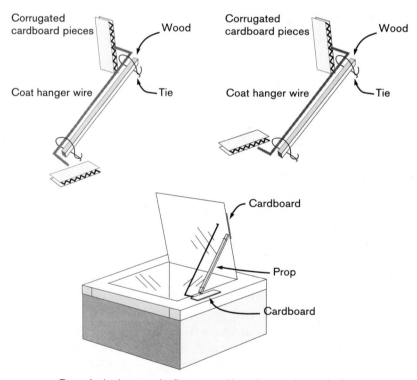

Props for both types of reflectors, and how the prop is attached

cooking with sunshine

window, bend the wire into an elongated Z shape; if your reflector is more nearly the width of the lid, bend the wire into an elongated U shape.

Glue pieces of corrugated cardboard to the reflector and the lid and insert the ends of the wire into the corrugations. Then tie the stick to the wire to keep it from buckling in a strong wind—the plastic cable ties found in electronics supply stores are ideal for this purpose. Note that it's important to put the prop on the side of the box shown in the illustration, which will be the side facing east when the cooker is facing south. If you put the prop on the side that will be facing west, its shadow will fall on the cooker as the sun progresses and slightly reduce the radiation entering the cooker.

And there you have it—your own solar box cooker. You might want to protect the outside with paint, wax, or contact paper to make it water resistant. Then stand back and congratulate yourself!

▶ BUILDING A PANEL COOKER

BEFORE YOU START to build your panel cooker, read all of the building instructions. Note that the sturdier the cardboard you use, the better. Sturdy panel cookers can last for years.

GATHER THE MATERIALS

To build your panel cooker, you'll need these materials:

- A **piece of cardboard** measuring 36 x 48 inches (91 x 122 cm)
- Enough **aluminum foil** to cover one side of the cardboard
- A **box-cutting knife or heavy shears** to cut the cardboard and foil
- A sturdy **straightedge** and **large spoon** or other rounded metal object to score the cardboard before creasing and folding it
- A **measuring tape, yardstick, or meter stick**, and a **pencil** to mark your measurements
- About 6 ounces of **water-soluble glue** such as Elmer's Glue-All[r]
- A **small container** in which to mix the glue with water
- An **old paintbrush** to spread the glue

MARK THE GUIDELINES

Lay the cardboard on a level surface with the long edge facing you. Then measure and mark vertical lines on the cardboard as shown. A carpenter's square can help when you draw the guidelines, but don't assume that the cardboard actually has square corners or exactly parallel opposite edges. The most accurate approach is to mark the same measurements on opposite edges of the cardboard, then connect the marks.

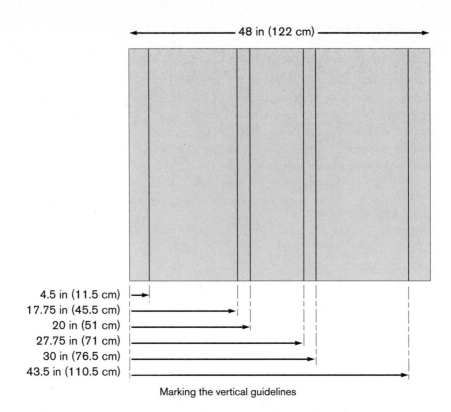

4.5 in (11.5 cm)
17.75 in (45.5 cm)
20 in (51 cm)
27.75 in (71 cm)
30 in (76.5 cm)
43.5 in (110.5 cm)

Marking the vertical guidelines

Then measure and mark horizontal lines on the cardboard as shown.

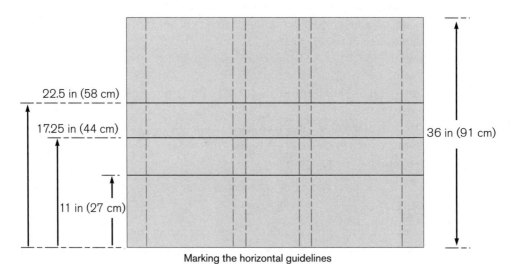

22.5 in (58 cm)

17.25 in (44 cm)

11 in (27 cm)

36 in (91 cm)

Marking the horizontal guidelines

MARK AND CUT THE PANEL AND SLOTS

Use your straightedge to mark off the cutouts as shown, keying off the guidelines you drew.

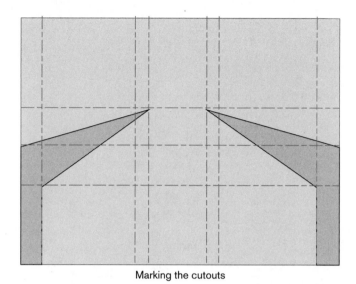

Marking the cutouts

Then use heavy shears or a box knife to cut away the indicated areas. Remember the carpenter's motto: measure twice, cut once!

Next, measuring as shown, mark and cut slots in the panel. The slots should be 4 to 5 inches (10 to 12 cm) long, and about the width of the cardboard's thickness.

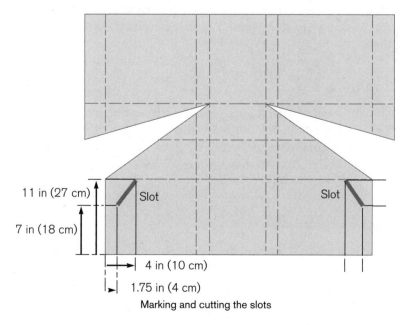

11 in (27 cm)

7 in (18 cm)

Slot

Slot

4 in (10 cm)

1.75 in (4 cm)

Marking and cutting the slots

building a solar cooker

Note that if you live at a high latitude (far from the equator, where the sun isn't as high in the sky), you can make the slots as long as practical and trim as much as necessary from the bottom edge of the upper wings to allow the back of the reflector to stand almost vertical.

SCORE THE PANEL

Mark four lines on the panel as shown.

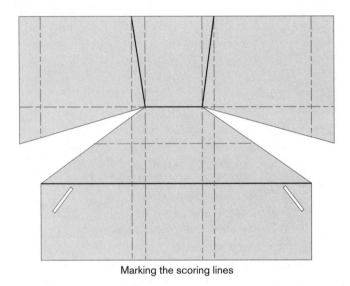

Marking the scoring lines

Then, using your straightedge and the edge of a smooth metal object like a large spoon, score the cardboard along the marks so it can be creased and folded easily, but don't fold it yet.

GLUE FOIL TO THE PANEL

Mix the glue with about two parts water and brush it onto a section of the panel. Then cover this surface with aluminum foil, gluing the shiny side to the panel so that the dull side is exposed. (Contrary to what you might expect, the diffusing property of the dull side has been shown to produce the best heating.) Work section by section, applying the foil before the glue dries.

FOLD AND SET UP THE COOKER

When the glue is dry, fold and set up the panel cooker as shown. Insert the corners of the back part of the reflector into the slots. If the fit of the slots isn't snug enough to hold the corners in place, fasten a spring clothespin or document clip to the corners underneath the base reflector to keep them from sliding out.

cooking with sunshine

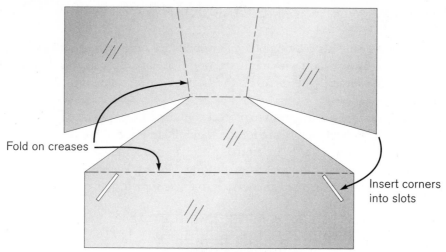

Fold on creases

Insert corners into slots

Folding and setting up the cooker

Your panel cooker is complete. To use it, place a dark cooking pot on an insulating spacer such as a thin piece of wood, a coil of rope, a wire standoff, or a brick. Enclose both the spacer and the pot in one of those high-temperature oven bags available at the grocery store (get a turkey-sized bag for maximum versatility) and place everything in the center of the bottom reflector. Keep it pointed at the sun, and you're cooking with sunshine!

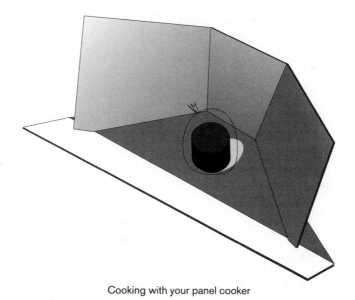

Cooking with your panel cooker

▶ MAKING A WIRE FRAME STANDOFF

INSTEAD OF SETTING your cooking pot on a wood block or brick in your box or panel cooker, you can easily make a wire frame standoff that not only insulates your cooking pot but also allows sunlight to reach the bottom surface, heating the pot from underneath.

You'll need a pair of sturdy gloves to protect your hands, and pliers to bend the wire. The best material we've found to use for the standoff is a piece of hardware cloth from our local hardware store. Hardware cloth is a coarse wire screen that's been dipped in solder to keep the warp and woof from shifting. Get a piece long enough to wrap around your favorite cooking pot and wrap it to fit, as shown.

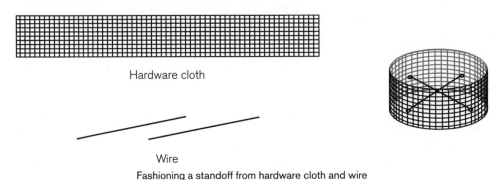

Hardware cloth

Wire

Fashioning a standoff from hardware cloth and wire

Secure the ends by bending the wires, and fold back any sharp protruding ends to protect your hands and to keep from puncturing the cooking bag. Fasten a pair of cross wires about an inch from the bottom of the wire frame to support the pot, and you're done.

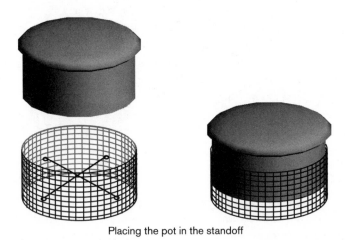

Placing the pot in the standoff

7

answers to further questions you may have

HERE YOU'LL FIND the answers to questions that beginning solar cooks commonly ask. If you don't find the answer to your own particular question here, try researching it on the Solar Cooking Archive at www.solarcooking.org, sponsored by Solar Cookers International (SCI). SCI serves as an information clearinghouse and can steer you in the right direction to find the answer you need. More information on how to contact SCI can be found in the Resources section.

Are there any health and safety concerns I should be aware of in solar cooking?
Yes. Parabolic cookers create a very hot focal point that's invisible but that can burn skin and eyes if someone inadvertently puts a limb or a face in this zone; moreover, if these cookers aren't stored properly out of the sunshine, their mirrors can actually start fires. Extreme caution should be used with these cookers.

Although the outside of a solar box or panel cooker doesn't get hot and thus doesn't pose a safety problem, you do need to stay aware that black cooking vessels get quite hot and should be handled with potholders. Food safety is also a concern and is covered in Chapter 1. One further concern is eye safety. Around any kind of solar reflector, flashes of intensified sunlight can hit the eyes. For this reason, you should get in the habit of approaching a solar cooker with your back to the sun so that your shadow blocks the sunlight. You can also wear sunglasses when you're doing solar cooking.

Why does food taste better when it's solar cooked?
Temperatures rise slowly and evenly in a cooking vessel placed in a solar panel or box cooker. This gives complex carbohydrates time to break down into simple sugars, allowing natural flavors and sweetness to emerge. Foods never scorch, because there are no hot spots. And meats cooked slowly at low temperatures have time to get more tender than when they're cooked quickly at high temperatures.

Does it really matter whether a cooker is made out of cardboard or some more durable material?

Cardboard cookers can't be left out in the rain, but aside from that, they work just as well as cookers made of more durable materials. They may not get as hot, topping out at around 300°F as food approaches being done, but you may prefer to cook your food at lower temperatures over a longer period of time anyway, especially if you're going to be gone all day and want to put your food in early and not worry about it overcooking. A cardboard cooker that's well cared for can last for ten years or more.

Would my box cooker get hotter if I painted the inside walls black or used more insulation in the walls?

The walls of your cooker will get hotter if you paint them black, but the food won't necessarily get hotter. Covering the walls with foil keeps the sunlight bouncing until it hits either the black pot or the optional dark bottom tray, both of which will result in more heat being delivered to your food. More insulation won't make much of a difference, because most of the heat loss in a box cooker is through the window on the top, not through the walls. Some people place only a piece of foiled cardboard in the walls as insulation, and this seems to do the job while keeping the cooker lighter.

You can increase the efficiency of your box cooker slightly by using glass instead of plastic for the window. Glass reportedly provides about 10 percent better performance than plastic, but plastic works plenty well if it's all you have on hand or if you need to make your cooker lighter and easier to transport.

Do I need to get an oven thermometer to use in solar cooking?

You might find an oven thermometer helpful in a couple of different circumstances. If you're trying to cook on a partly cloudy or a windy or cold day, a thermometer placed on your cooking vessel can let you know whether your food is reaching cooking temperatures (180°F). And if you're preheating your solar box cooker before baking bread or cake, a thermometer can tell you when the box has reached 300°F, a temperature some experienced solar cooks aim for before putting their baked goods in the box. Of course, the temperature will fall when you put the uncooked food in the box, but you still will have given it a head start. You may also want to use a meat thermometer if you're not sure about cooking times for meat and want to make sure that your meat is thoroughly cooked.

Should I stir food when it's cooking in the solar cooker?

In general, you don't need to stir food in a solar cooker. It's not necessary to prevent scorching, since there aren't any hot spots, and there are a couple of good reasons not to stir. For one thing, every time you open your cooker or oven bag and your pot, you let warm air escape, and this slows down the cooking. For another thing, stirring rice (in a solar cooker or on a stove) actually creates gumminess. It's best to leave this food undisturbed and to just poke a little hole down through the center if you need to find out whether all the liquid has been absorbed.

That said, some people using a panel cooker have reported that they need to stir food every once in a while to assure that the food heats evenly. This is because panel cookers can heat up faster than box cookers. This becomes less of a concern when you're not moving your panel cooker to follow the sun and are leaving a dish in all day to cook.

Do I need to worry about critters bothering my food when I'm using a solar cooker?

If you're cooking in your backyard, you don't need to worry. The lids on the pots keep the odor of food from reaching animals, and animals are really smart about avoiding hot objects. On the other hand, if you're cooking in a backcountry campground that bears frequent, you might want to keep an eye on your food until the cooking pot heats up.

Is there any way to speed up solar cooking?

Yes, you can keep temperatures higher by turning the cooker to follow the sun. You may want to do this if you're baking bread, cake, or cookies, or if you're cooking beans. A good rule of thumb is to plan to readjust the cooker every 30 minutes to maintain the highest temperatures. You can also amplify the heat by using more reflectors. See the answer to the next question for more on this method.

It's late in the season. Can I still use my solar cooker?

Solar cooking depends on gathering sufficient sunlight. This is harder when the angle of the sun is lower, in early spring, late fall, and winter, but it's still possible. One way to approach the problem of low-sun days is to mount additional reflectors to capture more sun. You can make additional reflectors out of cardboard and foil and attach them temporarily to your box cooker lid or to the back reflector of your panel cooker.

We've used a reflective Mylar auto windshield shade with success, held in place with document clamps on both panel and box cookers (see photo page 187). These shades are highly reflective, but because they're flexible you may need to support them in some way. In the photo of the box cooker below you can see that we've used hiking poles to hold up the outside corners of the windshield shade. The panel cooker provides enough support for the shade without any special help.

It's interesting to note that air temperature has little to do with whether you can successfully cook a meal with sunshine. Solar box cookers have been used with great success at the base of Mount Everest, where temperatures are often well below zero. Although there are more cooking hours available in the summer than in the winter, it's been proven that food will often cook faster on a clear, low-humidity day when the air temperature is 40°F than on a day in the 90s when humidity is high and haze cuts the brightness of the sun.

A box cooker with an additional reflector improvised from a windshield shade

It gets cloudy a lot in the summer where I live. Can I still cook with sunshine?
You can cook with sunshine as long as you get about twenty minutes of sunshine every hour. On a day when you think clouds might come in, you can attach additional reflectors to your cooker as described above, to gather more sunlight. If unpredictable cloudiness is a constant problem in your locale, you may want to invest in a hybrid cooker that uses electricity or gas to keep the cooker hot when the sun is weak. See the Resources section for a description of one such cooker.

I've already put my food in the solar cooker, and now it's gotten cloudy. What should I do?
Rig extra reflectors as described above, and then monitor your cooker to see how warm it's getting (put an oven thermometer on top of your cooking pot, for example). A surprising amount of solar energy still comes through on a cloudy day, but if you find that your cooker just won't heat, your only recourse is to bring the food inside and finish cooking conventionally. How long should you wait? Remember that you don't want partially cooked food—especially meats—to remain in the danger zone between 50°F and 125°F for more than three hours, so judge accordingly.

A panel cooker amplified with a windshield shade

I tried to bake a cake in my panel cooker, but the oven bag collapsed on top of the cake. The cake got done anyway, but the bag was stuck to its top. Is there anything I can do about this problem in the future?

The solar panel cooker was designed to cook food in a dark lidded pot. It's not impossible to cook food uncovered in a panel cooker, but it's awkward, as you've discovered. Try venting the oven bag as we've suggested elsewhere, by closing it with a twist tie wrapped around a sewing bobbin or some other small object with a hole in it. You may want to improvise some sort of wire frame to hold the bag up off the food you're cooking uncovered. See the instructions at the end of Chapter 6 for building a wire frame standoff for ideas about materials you might use.

Can the recipes in this book be prepared in an indoor oven?

Yes. To simulate solar cooking conditions and get the health and flavor benefits of cooking at lower temperatures, set your indoor oven at anywhere from 200°F to 250°F, depending on whether you're most interested in keeping the food really tender (the lower temperature) or getting it to brown or cook faster (the higher temperature). If you're most interested in speed, you can turn your oven to 325°F or 350°F and cut the cooking time in half.

Is there any other use for my solar cooker besides cooking food?

Yes. The solar cooker can be used to can fruits (but not vegetables or meats, which need to be canned under pressure) and to sterilize potting soil, grains, or surgical instruments. It can also be used to boil and pasteurize water. Water should be held at 150°F for 20 minutes to pasteurize it and kill all human disease pathogens. The water doesn't have to reach boiling (212°F), although boiling does serve as a visible temperature indicator if you have no other way of telling how hot the water is. Solar Cookers International (SCI) sells a little device called a water pasteurization indicator or WAPI that tells you when water has been held at a sufficient temperature for long enough to pasteurize it. See the Resources section for information on how to order from SCI.

The solar cooker can also be used as a cooler. Steven E. Jones and his student Jamie Winterton at Brigham Young University were among the first to demonstrate this effect. They had the idea that their panel-style cooker in the shape of a funnel could be used effectively to shield their cooking jar from surrounding warm objects at night. Objects like buildings and trees trap the heat of the day and radiate it away after sunset. By pointing the funnel cooker toward the dark night sky and away from buildings and trees, the two discovered that the jar actually became colder than the surrounding temperature. The cold of outer space acted as a heat sink, and the warmth of the jar radiated speedily away in the form of infrared energy. They put water in the jar and, on a night when the outdoor temperature never dipped below 47.5°F, they made ice.

You can try this for yourself by finding a suitably large piece of cardboard, cutting a semicircle along one edge, shaping it into a funnel, and lining it with reflective foil. Set it up pointing at the northern sky and place water in a black jar inside the funnel. Wrap the jar in a plastic bag to insulate it from the surrounding air. The BYU researchers recommend using polyethylene bags instead of oven cooking bags because they're more transparent to infrared radiation—and of course, there's no danger of their melting. For best effect, they recommend using two bags instead of just one. Note that box cookers with glass lids don't work very well for this application—the glass blocks most infrared radiation, so a dark pot inside the oven won't lose its heat effectively.

resources

▶ WHERE CAN YOU BUY A SOLAR COOKER?

READY-MADE SOLAR cookers can be ordered from catalogs ranging from the sturdy Amish Lehman's in Ohio (www.lehmans.com) to the ecologically oriented Real Goods catalog (www.realgoods.com) to the upscale Hammacher Schlemmer (www.hammacher.com) in New York. They range in price from the very affordable CooKit and Suntoys solar cookers ($20–$25 range) to the pricey European design found in the Hammacher Schlemmer catalog ($299), with the SOS Sport and the Global Sun Oven somewhere in between. You can also order directly from the sources shown below.

THE COOKIT
The CooKit is a lightweight cardboard panel cooker that's convenient for home, camping, and emergencies. It reaches temperatures in the mid-200°s Fahrenheit and folds flat to 13 x 13 x 2 inches. Two high-temperature cooking bags, required for cooking, are included with it. Use it with a black lidded pot, not included but also for sale from Solar Cookers International. Your purchases support solar cooking education worldwide.

Solar Cookers International
1919 21st Street, Suite 101
Sacramento, CA 95814
(916) 455-4499
info@solarcookers.org
www.solarcooking.org

THE SUNTOYS SOLAR COOKER

The Suntoys solar cooker developed by David Piper is a reflective panel cooker just like the CooKit except that it's made of crushable, water-resistant foam. It holds up in wet weather but needs staking in the wind. Available from Solar Cookers International (www.solarcooking.org), Lehman's (www.lehmans.com), or David Piper.

David Piper
Suntoys Solar Cookers
P. O. Box 622
Renton, WA 98055
(206) 230-5286
davidpiper@usa.net

THE HOTPOT SIMPLE SOLAR COOKER

The HotPot Simple Solar Cooker consists of a black 5.3-quart enameled steel pot supported inside a clear tempered glass bowl, resting inside a collapsible aluminum reflector. It was developed by Solar Household Energy (SHE), Inc., whose mission is "to harness free enterprise for the introduction of solar cooking to improve quality of life and relieve stress on the environment." HotPots for individual use can be purchased from the Real Goods catalog (www.realgoods.com). Those considering using the HotPot in international projects should contact SHE directly.

Solar Household Energy, Inc.
P. O. Box 15063
Chevy Chase, MD 20825
inquiries@SHE-inc.org
www.she-inc.org

THE SOS SPORT

The lightweight plastic SOS Sport Solar Oven, developed by Mike and Martha Port of the Solar Oven Society with help from retired 3M engineers and made mostly of recycled pop bottles, reaches temperatures of 210°F to 270°F without reflectors and up to 350°F when placed in full sun with the optional reflectors. The Sport weighs 10 pounds and measures 12 x 27 x 17 inches. The clever design allows you to set the oven on its back to catch more sun during the winter. The Sport comes with two cooking pots, an oven thermometer, a water pasteurization indicator, and an instruction booklet. Every Sport purchased in the U.S. helps offset the cost of sending solar ovens to developing countries. It's available from the Solar Oven Society.

Solar Oven Society
3225 East Hennepin Avenue, Suite 200
Minneapolis, MN 55413
(612) 623-4700
FAX (612) 623-3311
sos@solarovens.org
www.solarovens.org

THE GLOBAL SUN OVEN

The Global Sun Oven is a high-performance, durable solar box cooker made of molded plastic. It reaches temperatures of 360°F to 400°F, weighs 21 pounds, and measures 19 x 19 x 11 inches. It's available from the manufacturer (Sun Ovens International), from Solar Cookers International (www.solarcooking.org), and from Real Goods (www.real-goods.com) and Lehman's (www.lehmans.com). Sun Ovens International also makes a larger model, called the Villager Sun Oven, which can handle large quantities of food for institutions and bakeries. Their motto is "Saving lives by preserving forests around the world."

> Sun Ovens International
> 39W835 Midan Drive
> Elburn, IL 60119
> (800) 408-7919
> info@sunoven.com
> www.sunoven.com

THE SUN COOK SOLAR OVEN

The heaviest, most expensive, and perhaps most stylish of the solar cookers currently available, this model was designed in Portugal. The Sun Cook solar oven weighs 30 pounds, measures 11.5 x 22 x 23 inches, and reaches temperatures of 400°F. It's made of molded plastic, aluminum, and tempered glass and has integral handles for easy toting. It includes cooking pot, roasting pan, instructions, and recipes. Call Hammacher Schlemmer customer service at 1-800-321-1484 regarding this product's availability if you can't find it on their Web site (www.hammacher.com, where it's advertised as "The European Solar Oven"). Or contact the manufacturer (www.sun-co.pt) directly at sales@sun-co.pt.

THE SOLAREFLEX 900 COOKER

This unique concentrator-type solar cooker attains temperatures comparable to a toaster oven and is at its best cooking in the winter, according to its inventor, Deris Jeannette. For details and to order, visit the Web site at www.cleardomesolar.com or contact:

> Deris Jeannette
> ClearDome Solar
> 3368 Governor Drive, 153-F
> San Diego, CA 92122
> (619) 990-7977
> cleardomesolar@sbcglobal.net

THE TULSI-HYBRID SOLAR COOKING OVEN

This molded plastic oven reaches temperatures of more than 350°F, folds up like a suitcase for easy portability, and has a low-wattage electric backup for cloudy and partly cloudy days. Available from the Sunbd Corporation at www.sunbdcorp.com.

►WHERE CAN YOU GET MORE RECIPES?

A VARIETY OF solar cookery books have been published over the years. These four books are available from Solar Cookers International (www.solarcooking.org) and online booksellers:

- *The Solar Cookbook: Recipes for a Sun-Cooked Diet* by Stella Andrassy (1981) details her experiences as a pioneer in solar cooking research, describes how to build a solar box cooker she calls a SUNNET Sunstove, and includes a range of recipes for omnivores.

- *Solar Cooking: A Primer/Cookbook* by Harriet Kofalk (1993) tells how to build a simple solar box cooker and offers a couple dozen vegetarian recipes.

- *Solar Cooking Naturally* by Virginia Heather Gurley (3rd edition, 1995) includes a variety of recipes for vegetarian and omnivorous diets.

- *Cooking with the Sun* by Beth and Dan Halacy (1992, revised edition of *The Solar Cookery Book*, 1978) tells how to build two cookers they designed: a plywood solar oven that can reach a temperature of 400°F and a solar hot plate capable of frying bacon and eggs. A variety of recipes for these cookers is included.

These two books are available from the publishers, as indicated:

- *Eleanor's Solar Cookbook* by Eleanor Shimeall (Cemese Publishers, P. O. Box 1022, Borrego Springs, CA 92004, 1983) focuses on a traditional American diet and has an especially good section on canning fruit and tomatoes in the solar box cooker.

- *The Morning Hill Solar Cookery Book* by Jennifer Stein Barker (Morning Hill Associates, HC 84 Box 632, Canyon City, OR 97820, 1999) contains a range of healthful vegetarian recipes along with vignettes from the solar homestead in eastern Oregon that Jennifer shares with her husband, Lance.

►WHERE CAN YOU FIND OUT MORE ABOUT SOLAR COOKING?

THE SOLAR COOKING Archive hosted by Solar Cookers International (www.solarcooking.org) is a great source of further information about solar cooking. These books are available there:

- *The Expanding World of Solar Box Cookers* by Barbara Kerr (1991) focuses on the history, theory, and patterns of solar box cooker use worldwide. It discusses non-cooking uses and gives detailed plans and instructions for building four different models. Especially valuable for educators.

- *Heaven's Flame: A Guidebook to Solar Cookers* by Joseph Radabaugh (2nd edition, 1998) provides a thorough discussion of solar oven design considerations and tells how to build an oven of Radabaugh's own design, the SunStar. This book is also available from www.amazon.com.

- *Making the Most of Sunshine: A Handbook of Solar Energy for the Common Man* by S. Narayanaswami discusses solar cooking in the context of environmental concerns, describes several types of solar cookers, and gives instructions for building a solar box cooker.

A video showing the major components of a sustainable home, plus a comprehensive plan for off-grid cooking called "The Sustainable Kitchen," as well as solar cooker plans and other resources, are available from:

The Kerr-Cole Sustainable Living Center
P. O. Box 576 (mailing address)
3310 Paper Mill Road (street address)
Taylor, AZ 85939
(928) 536-2269 or (928) 536-5123
kerrcole@frontiernet.net or scottjl@onewave.com

▶ HOW CAN YOU SUPPORT THE SPREAD OF SOLAR COOKING?

IF YOU'RE LOOKING for a way to help people and environments around the world, supporting the spread of solar cooking is a good place to put your money or volunteer skills. Solar cooking is a great help to people facing firewood shortages. It frees them from the need to cut down trees or go on an arduous daily trek of many miles to find wood. It also offers them a simple way to sterilize contaminated drinking water, thus greatly improving sanitary conditions. Here are three organizations doing great work that you might want to consider giving to:

- Solar Cookers International "assists communities to use the power of the sun to cook food and pasteurize water for the benefit of people and environments." Founded in 1987 as Solar Box Cookers International, this organization is spreading the gospel of solar cooking in developing nations. You'll get their quarterly newsletter if you join.

Solar Cookers International
1919 21st Street, Suite 101
Sacramento, CA 95814
(916) 455-4499
info@solarcookers.org
www.solarcooking.org

■ Solar Household Energy (SHE), Inc., aims "to harness free enterprise for the introduction of solar cooking to improve quality of life and relieve stress on the environment." It identifies, supports, and promotes entrepreneurs, nongovernmental organizations, and public entities in the developing world who manufacture or market solar ovens. Your financial support will enable it to undertake new solar cooker distribution projects.

Solar Household Energy, Inc.
P. O. Box 15063
Chevy Chase, MD 20825
inquiries@SHE-inc.org
www.she-inc.org

■ The Solar Oven Society "exists to promote solar cooking to the American public and to provide a way to partner with the over 2 billion people worldwide who lack adequate fuel for cooking their food." Purchases of the SOS Sport and donations to SOS help subsidize the cost of sending the SOS Sport to Third World countries.

Solar Oven Society
3225 East Hennepin Avenue, Suite 200
Minneapolis, MN 55413
(612) 623-4700
FAX (612) 623-3311
sos@solarovens.org
www.solarovens.org

conversion table

IT HAS COME to our attention that not everyone is familiar with the quaint units of measure we use in the United States. If you're used to a more rational system of weights and measures, this table is for you.

US UNITS	METRIC UNITS (approximate)
1 fluid ounce	30 ml
1 cup	240 ml
1 teaspoon	5 ml
1 tablespoon	15 ml
1 quart	950 ml
1 pint	425 ml
1 ounce	28 g
1 pound	454 g
200°F	93°C
212°F	100°C
250°F	121°C
300°F	150°C
1 inch	2.54 cm
1 foot	29.4 cm

acknowledgments

ONE OF THE joys of solar cooking for us has been the generous, good-hearted people it's brought us into contact with. We're particularly grateful to the staff of Solar Cookers International, Barbara Kerr, Sherry Cole, and the Sacramento Municipal Utility District for getting us started with solar cooking. We owe special thanks to Beverly Blum, executive director of SCI; Scott Chaplin, senior research associate, Rocky Mountain Institute; and to Bud Clevett, Sherry Cole, Barbara Kerr, and Betti Paver for helpful comments on early drafts of the book. Many thanks to Laurence Taoman and Kevin "Rex" Anderson for perceptive comments on the current version.

Thanks to Kerr-Cole Enterprises for permission to disseminate the solar box cooker plans. Barbara Kerr's *The Expanding World of Solar Box Cookers*, Joseph Radabaugh's *Heaven's Flame: A Guidebook to Solar Cookers*, and Beth and Dan Halacy's *Cooking with the Sun* provided us with basic information, as did "Solar Cooker" by Edwin Dobb in the November–December 1992 issue of *Audubon*, and Barbara Knudson's report on solar cooking around the world (www.she-inc.org). We gathered further ideas and inspiration from the Solar Cooking Archive (www.solarcooking.org) and from a number of different cookbooks, both solar and conventional, including *Eleanor's Solar Cookbook* by Eleanor Shimeall, *Solar Cooking Naturally* by Virginia Heather Gurley, *Sol Food* and *Solar Cooking: A Primer/Cookbook* by Harriet Kofalk, *The Morning Hill Solar Cookery Book* by Jennifer Stein Barker, *The Solar Cookbook* by Stella Andrassy, *The Windstar Feast Cookbook* by Diane Sturgis, *The Victory Garden Cookbook* by Marian Morash, *Moosewood Restaurant Cooks at Home* by the Moosewood Collective, *The Savory Way* by Deborah Madison, *The Natural Health Cookbook* by Dana Jacobi et al., *The Crockery Cook* by Mable Hoffman, and *Cooking Without Fuel* by Julia Older.

Thanks also to Audrey Anderson, Wilma Anderson, Claudia Schulz, Helen James, Claire Marie Palkovic, Caroline Rose, Pauline Hoopes, Tom Shessler, John Wagner,

Priscilla High, and Susan Cockrell for contributing recipes. Thanks to Anna Joy Thigpen Hunt, Kathy Williams, Pauline Hoopes, and Laurence Taoman for testing and commenting on recipes.

Thanks to Jonathan Reynolds for quoting us in his article "Sunny Side Up," which appeared in the August 21, 2005, issue of the *New York Times Magazine*, bringing solar cooking to the attention of a wider audience and of our publisher, Matthew Lore. And thanks to the crew at Marlowe & Company who ably transformed our self-published book into the tome you hold in your hands, particularly our editor, Peter Jacoby.

index

potatoes, 118–19
  salad, 112, 120, 122
pots, 7–10
poultry, 56–72
proscuitto, 53
pudding, 115, 145, 151
pumpkin, 132, 148
puree, 121

Q

quiche, 35, 55
quinoa, 92–93

R

Radabaugh, Joseph, 193
radiation, 3
raspberry sauce, 150
ratatouille, 45
reflector cookers, xi, 10–11
refried beans, 100
refrigerator cookies, 15
rice, 82, 84–88, 95
roll-ups, 68
rosemary, 86

S

Sacramento Municipal Utility District
  (SMUD), xviii
safety of food, 5–6, 183
salads
  almond, 92
  barley, 92
  brown rice, 88
  chicken, 57–60
  lentils, 102
  potato, 112, 120, 122
  quinoa, 93
  véronique, 57
salmon, 49–50
sausage, 21
scallops, 54
seafood, 47–55

seeds, 18
sesame seeds, 120
shallots, 54
Shimeall, Eleanor, 192
shrimp, 53
slow cooker recipes, 5
s'mores, 15
The Solar Cook Book, xix
*The Solar Cookbook: Recipes for a Sun-
  Cooked Diet*, 192
Solar Cookers International (SCI), 183,
  192–93, xv, xvii, xviii
The Solar Cookery Book, xix, 192
solar cooking, ix–xx
  building a cooker, 162–82
  buying a cooker, 189–91
  cooking times, 11–12, 185
  cookware, 7–10
  as coolers, 188
  design, xvii
  history of, xviii–xix
  temperature points, 6, 27, 184
  using cookers, 1–5, 10–11, 185
  See also cookers
Solar Cooking: A Primer/Cookbook, 192
Solar Cooking Archive, 183
Solar Cooking Naturally, 192
Solar Household Energy (SHE), Inc., 194
Solar Oven Society, 190, 194
solar radiation, 3
Solarflex 900 Cooker, 191
sole amandine, 52
SOS Sport Solar Oven, 10, 190
soup, 25
spinach, 120
squash, 121, 144
stew, 43, 70, 75, 80
stuffing, 69
sun tea, 14
sunlight, xvi
Suntoys solar cooker, 190
The Sustainable Kitchen, 193